THE SAILING SHIPS
OF GREAT BRITAIN

The pride of Henry VIII's navy – the *Henry
Grace à Dieu*, commonly known as the *Great
Harry*. She was built in 1514 to meet the ever-
threatening menace of Spain and was
destroyed by fire before having the opportunity
to prove herself in battle. See Plate II.

THE SAILING SHIPS OF GREAT BRITAIN

W. S. Hill

JUPITER BOOKS LONDON 1975

JUPITER BOOKS (LONDON) LIMITED
167 Hermitage Road, London N4.
Copyright © Jupiter Books (London) Limited 1975.
Printed by Jayprint Limited, Leicester.
SBN 904041 190
The publishers wish to thank Roy Allen for his
help in preparing the text of this volume, and
Paul White and the Mary Evans Collection for
permission to reproduce illustrations.

The full-rigged splendour of the racing clippers
in the 1860s. Such sights were common in the
second half of the nineteenth century when
every voyage was seen as a challenge. 'Who
will be the first to Bristol with this month's
essential oils?'

CONTENTS

The richly-decorated stern of a British man-of-war. Note particularly the three lanterns above and flanking the robust Royal arms. Ornamental work such as this characterized much ship-building in the seventeenth century.

INTRODUCTION

IT WAS A HEROIC TIME, a historic time, a magnificent and splendid time. The period in history when British ships evolved from the ordinary and workmanlike form they had assumed for many years and flowered into tall, fast and sometimes fearful craft equipped with skilled crews dedicated to mastering the seas and affirming that they could outsail and outshine their contemporaries from any other nation.

This chapter in Britain's seafaring history was as much a magnificent time as it was a hard time, although it would have been difficult to convince seaman then of its wonders. Men went to sea for a variety of reasons, most of them unrelated to the glory attached to the life by those who have never experienced it. They went to sea because they were runaways, because they were press-ganged into doing so, because if offered a livelihood (of sorts) and, most rarely of all, because they liked ships. Often men joined because their fathers before them had done so. Few thought of the sea as a career which led to profitable positions. Such aspirations came later, when Britain's navy was the most powerful in the world and her mercantile fleets the life-blood of world trade.

It was a hard life in the age of sail, and the life-expectancy was low. Men who went to sea stood a good chance of ill-health in their later years with rheumatism, arthritis and a host of other ailments which we now recognise but which then had not even been identified. In many cases seamen were hardly the most easily-treated of individuals – their life was, in its essence, hard and it was a matter of being fit for the job or not. This was the life, and men went along with it. They neither expected much comfort nor

did they get it, but in many cases, and on so many occasions, a seafarer's life could be exhilarating, for there was another side to the coin; the ship was a developing vehicle, it was becoming continually better and as it improved it was easier to handle and capable of ranging ever-farther across the seas, thus the seaman became more committed and dedicated to the life he had chosen.

So it was the seaman learned and came to love the stories and the sea shanties, and the ballads with them, and the world gained from this a chronicle of the splendid life there could be for the man of humble origins and little opportunity. Life itself was rigorous in the age of sail, and romance the preserve of the leisured classes. Hard work and danger offered, at the same time, opportunity for travel to fabled countries – a prospect not to be turned away from coldly. The sea to the young man of two or three hundred years ago held a similar attraction to that which the air would exert on the young flyers at the dawn of the twentieth century.

Out of this came ships, magnificent ships, ships which began in the same forms as in other lands: small exploratory vessels, piloted by their unskilled constructors, edging tentatively around the coasts of the British Isles, and developing through merchantmen and fiighting vessels to the great sailing ships which carried merchant cargoes speedily across the world in the interests of trade. Some of the ships built in England were the finest ever to sail the seas, and their story is the story of a great maritime nation.

THE VERY EARLY DAYS

The art of shipbuilding in the fifteenth century was confined to a
small band of shipyard foremen who reigned supreme over their
yards. These simple shipwrights worked according to tried and
trusted methods handed down from father to son. Ships were not
built by following carefully drawn-up plans and the essential
relationship between the vessel and her rigging was not yet fully
understood. The square body formed the basis on which
shipwrights established other co-ordinating elements. The keel, the
rudder-post at the stern and the stem-post at the bow defined the
skeleton on which the ribs would be placed.

Each master shipwright had his own trade secrets, with his ideas
written in a carefully guarded notebook. Some of these
manuscripts have survived, the famous *Construction of Galleys* dated
1410 and written by a Venetian is one such example.

In England, Henry V first used ships to transport his armies
across the Channel, and these ships were slow and cumbersome
and merely transport vessels. Eventually the military advantages
were recognised and ships became armed. Later, Henry VIII, who
founded the naval fighting force, took a keen interest in the
organization of his Royal Navy. He kept closely in touch with the
latest developments in Continental shipyards, going to great
lengths to obtain information from Venice on a type of 'galleon
driven by oars'. He also looked for a new use for his
'merchant-galleys' as by this time almost all of them were lying
idle, a result of the Mediterranean's decline in economic
importance now that the new trade routes led round the Cape of
Good Hope.

One of Henry VIII's ships was the 450-ton *Grand Mistress,*
described as a 'large-galleon' but classed as a 'galleass'. She was in
fact a hybrid vessel, her stern had the appearance of a galleon and
her bows were similar to a galley. The rigging was mixed with
square sails on the first two masts, and triangular lateen sails on the
mizzen and bonaventure mizzen-masts.

Henry VIII spent more money on ships of war than any other
king in Europe, and one of these was the *Great Harry.* Losing his
ship *Regent* in a fire in 1512 (it had been built by his father Henry
VII), Henry VIII immediately ordered the construction of another
and far larger ship, the *Great Carrack.* She was to bear several
different names – *Imperial Carrack, Henry Imperial* and finally,
Henry Grace à Dieu – but she is generally known as the *Great Harry.*
She was the pride of Henry's fleet, and the king attended her
launching, together with state and church dignitaries, and foreign
ambassadors to the English Court. The ship flew the green and
white flags of the House of Tudor and its splendid appearance
seemed to herald the beginning of England's new naval power.

For all its splendour the *Great Harry* had serious defects. The
excessive height of her topsides caused the ship to roll dreadfully in
high seas, and in 1536 the height of the vessel was reduced and her
tonnage fell from 1,500 to 1,000 tons. In her modified form the
ship's complement comprised more than 800 men, made up of
sailors, soldiers and gunners. She was armed with 21 bronze
cannon and had 130 smaller-calibre guns distributed over her four
lower decks, while yet more guns pointed from the decks of the
castles. A contemporary record shows that the rebuilt *Great Harry*

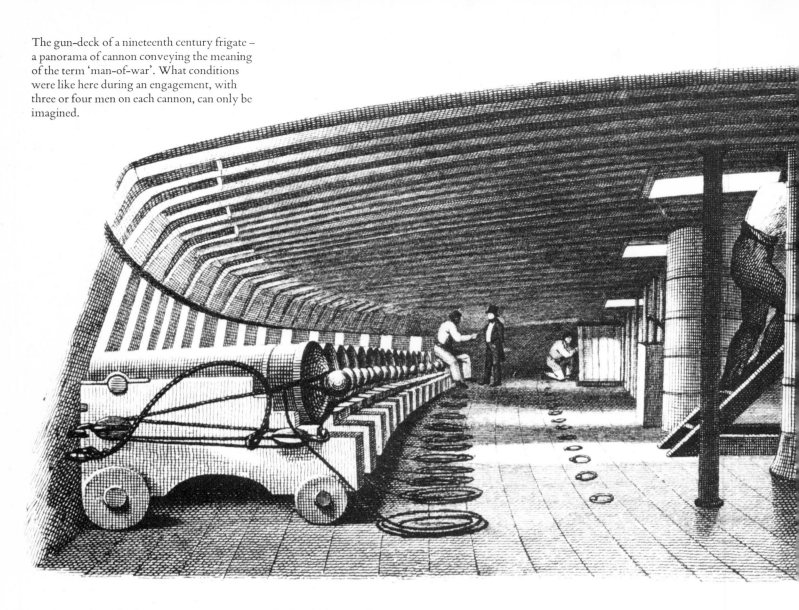

The gun-deck of a nineteenth century frigate –
a panorama of cannon conveying the meaning
of the term 'man-of-war'. What conditions
were like here during an engagement, with
three or four men on each cannon, can only be
imagined.

was rigged with four towering masts, each divided into three
sections. This was a new innovation permitting a more rational
spread of the total sail area. The foremast carried foresail,
fore-topsail and fore-topgallant, while the mainmast was rigged
with mainsail, main-topsail and topgallant. The two other masts,
incorrectly termed mizzen and bonaventure mizzen, carried five
triangular lateen sails between them. There were also large
gappling hooks at the end of the main-yards to grip the rigging of
an enemy ship and hold her firm during boarding.

The *Great Harry* did not have the opportunity to show her
might, she was destroyed by fire in Woolwich in 1553. Henry's
efforts in building a navy laid the foundations for a first-class sea
force, however, and later, by the time Elizabeth I was on the
throne, she was mistress of the most powerful navy Europe had
ever seen, with 18 powerful galleons, the smallest of which was
300 tons.

The time of Queen Elizabeth led to the development of the
fighting ship in its then most agressive form, and captains of
Elizabeth's navy sailed off to do battle and grab treasures in ships
that were to become famous.

Sir Francis Drake's ship *Golden Hind* was one that earned such a
place in history. Originally called *Pelican,* the ship weighed 240
tons and was one of a flotilla of five ships Drake assembled to
frighten Spanish merchant shipping from the Pacific Ocean. Drake
rounded Cape Horn in the ship and lost all of the accompanying
vessels in terrible weather during the attempt. He then sailed
north, up the coast of Chile and Peru, to return to Europe and
England by way of the Indian Ocean and Cape of Good Hope.

Queen Elizabeth subsequently knighted Drake in Plymouth in
September 1580.

Towards the end of the sixteenth century new ideas on ship
design were developing and important changes were made to hulls
and rigs. The ship's decoration increased in direct proportion to
the greater size of the vessel. On the galleons of the time the stern
of the ship was now flat, not rounded, and it became the general
practice for ships to display the picture of a saint together with the
heraldic arms of the royal family or the shipowner. Such
decorations were already well in evidence on Elizabethan ships
like the *Ark Royal* which was richly embossed with carved motifs.
Ships of European nations carried increasingly elaborate
decorations, the theme being repeated over the entire vessel and
terminating in a large carving at the prow on the cutwater. Female
figures and heraldic beasts were favourite subjects too with
maritime artists. Unfortunately, their artistic creations were
doomed to a brief existence, for if they escaped the ravages of
storms or enemy broadsides, they were generally smashed to pieces
by the wrecker's hammer when the ship was sent to the breaker's
yard.

THE BATTLE FLEETS

During the first thirty years of the seventeenth century, the
modern concept of the battle fleet emerged for the first time.
Powerful men-of-war, heavily armed with cannon, were needed
in quantity and the task of supplying this demand changed the face

of shipbuilding. The empiric methods of the small shipyards with their limited equipment and expertise were unable to cope with the new problems which constantly arose. Shipyards and foundries had to expand, new skills had to be learned and a production system evolved, and in that process shipbuilding became one of the first of modern industries.

The prime requirement was for shipbuilding materials, particularly wood. Oak was needed for hulls, pine for masts, poplar for ornamental carvings and elm for the gun mounts. Each maritime nation jealously guarded its sources of supply.

In England, all oak trees were reserved for the Royal Navy. The counties of Essex, Sussex and Hampshire yielded the best quality but these local sources were insufficient to meet the demands of the shipyards, and so wood was brought from the colonies in New England and the West Indies. The shipyard's appetite for oak was enormous; it took some 4,000 oak trees to produce a ship of 110 guns.

The construction of ships called for quantities of curved wood, and in England the wood was shaped to produce a sweeping curve in troughs of boiling water; the Dutch however favoured a type of steam bath. Copper and iron nails and bolts were sometimes used to secure joints, but in general the British and Dutch preferred to use wooden pegs or trennels for those parts of the hull which were below the water-line, because when iron rusted it rotted the surrounding wood.

After planking, the seams had to be caulked. Cracks were plugged with strands of oakum and then filled with melted pitch, and this in turn was overlaid with thick tar.

Once the construction of the hull had reached the stage when it would float, it was launched. Generally the ship was put into the water when the second deck was laid and the deadworks had risen as far as the second gundeck. This method was used in France and Holland and some Dutch shipbuilders kept the hull partly submerged under water for a year believing that this strengthened the wood, prevented residual sap from fermenting and gave the ship a longer working life.

The British, on the other hand, only launched their ships when the hull was completed and the interior fitted-out with the deadworks in place. A ship of 110 cannon took between three and four years to build. Extreme care was taken to ensure that the wood was absolutely free of sap, thereby minimizing its tendency to warp. In the early stages of construction it was sometimes necessary to allow six to eight months for the sap to drain from the frames before the planks were fastened on to them. Launching methods varied, the British ship was always launched stern first.

Fitting out was continued after the hull was afloat. Superstructures were added and the masts stepped deep into the bottom of the hold, this tricky operation requiring powerful hoisting gear. Once in place the masts were stayed by shrouds. The construction of the ship completed, she received her suit of sails and was ready for service. It was the responsibility of the officers in command to trim their vessels until the best sailing qualities were obtained from her.

The beginning of the sixteenth century saw the move westward across the seas to what was the New World – America. The now famous *Mayflower* presaged the flow of ships from Europe in later

years. She set sail for her most famous voyage in September 1620 carrying 101 passengers, sixty-six of them English, thirty-five Dutch. They landed in the New World in November 1620, by which time half of their number had died.

The various European maritime nations built their ships in different ways, but during the seventeenth century the British were recognized as the world's master shipbuilders. An account written in 1672 notes 'the British vessels stand out from those of other nations for the sturdiness, artistry and grace of their construction...' British hulls were sleeker, the topsides lighter and the general shape more hydrodynamic. The great improvements in ship design of this period meant that ships were more seaworthy, they rolled and pitched less and were better rigged.

The arrangements of the ports allowed more cannon to be carried on board. British ships also had more spacious galleys and the pulleys, capstans and anchors were all of excellent quality. The superior quality of British ship construction was such that in 1785 a French sea captain wrote, 'A British ship built today is in every respect a model of perfection; the finish and strength of her construction, the care and work lavished on all that goes into her have endowed her with such advantages that no comparison can be made with anything put to the same use in ships of other nations.' Visitors to British shipyards admired the good organization and the methods practised. Each ship under construction had its own stores which housed all the materials and tools necessary for its completion. The excellence of ship construction contributed greatly to the success of the British fleet during the eighteenth century and the Empire period.

A new development came from Britain in 1774. It was the carronade, a light, quick-firing gun initially intended for the defence of merchant-ships against pirates. The carronade, usually cast in Scotland, was capable of firing cannon-balls or charges of grapeshot at the rate of one in three minutes, and it needed only three gunners to man it. The carronade was adopted by the British Navy in 1779 and proved very effective against ships' crews and rigging. It was well suited to the armament of smaller craft, although it could not replace heavy guns on large ships because of its inadequate range and penetration.

This was the time of Nelson and of his ship, the *Victory,* which had been commissioned by the Admiralty in 1758 as a three-masted, three-decked gunboat. The *Victory* was christened in October 1760 and the hull completed by May 1765 when she was floated out of the dock at Chatham. She was made the flagship of Admiral Keppel, and as England was at war with France again by 1777 she joined the fleet, firing her guns for the first time in July 1778. There were 100 guns, in three complete tiers, 42-pounders, 24-pounders, and 12-pounders and 6-pounders. The ship became the flagship of Lord Howe in 1782, and in the war of the French Revolution she served Lord Hood. In 1796 she was once more a flagship, under Admiral of the Fleet, Sir John Jervis, and then she was taken out of service to exist for a time as a prison-hulk at Chatham. In 1799 the *Victory* was re-introduced into service, however, and in 1803 in the Mediterranean she flew the flag of Lord Nelson. Two years later, in October 1805, the *Victory* engaged the French at the Battle of Trafalgar where Lord Nelson was fatally wounded.

In 1821 the *Victory* was berthed in the dry-dock at Portsmouth to serve as an historical monument and museum. She remains there until this day, a fitting tribute to England's maritime glory.

Throughout this period the disposition of armament remained virtually the same. Ships were equipped with light arms such as perriers, which were small guns placed in the tops or quarter-decks and mounted on a pivoting fork. They were capable of fairly quick fire and proved effective at close range. Additionally, squads of men armed with muskets were trained to fire at close quarters on enemy ships. (It was a ball from a musket that killed Nelson at Trafalgar). Side arms were also carried to be used by the boarding parties.

Cannon were placed between decks along the length of the ship, firing through gunports which were closed with deadlights when not in use. Heavy pieces, such as the 24- and 36-pound guns were placed on the lowest batteries for stability. Although having the heaviest fire-power, these guns were located so close to the water-line that they were sometimes swamped by high seas or when the ship heeled over during manoeuvres. This was not an unusual occurrence, and more than once it had tragic consequences. Two hundred years earlier, in 1545, one of Henry's ships, the *Mary Rose* was lost with 400 men on board when she attempted a sharp turn in narrow waters off Ryde, Isle of Wight, because the gunports were left open. That wreck, incidentally, is still there today, and in 1970 plans were mooted to raise the wreck and salvage her, but so far she remains held fast.

Upper batteries and the quarter-decks were armed with lighter guns, the calibres decreasing progressively towards the top deck.

During the seventeenth century light cannon were often installed in the bows and stern for action in pursuit or retreat, but this proved ineffective and the arrangement was abandoned. No major changes were made to the disposition of the guns until the latter half of the nineteenth century.

After 1760 maritime discovery moved ahead with the exploration of the Pacific, primarily by the French and English, which marked the beginning of scientific charting and surveying as we know it today. Improvements in shipbuilding and design made conditions on board more bearable and hygenic for the crews and for the scientists and scholars who journeyed with them.

EVOLUTION IN SHIP DESIGN

The great sailing ship reigned for two and a half centuries. Coming into prominence early in the seventeenth century the sailing man-of-war and merchantman gradually replaced the galley until the great rise of steam propulsion shortly after 1850.

The advantages of the sailing ship over the galley were enormous. The galley was essentially a Mediterranean craft with a limited range. It was low on the water and unsuited to long voyages in rough seas, and in battle the galley was no match for the sailing man-of-war. Nonetheless the galley survived until the eighteenth century.

The great sailing-ships first appeared about 1630. The *Sovereign of the Seas,* a British ship built in 1627, was the first of a long line. Apart from the elongated beak under the bowsprit, inherited from

the galley prow, and a sterncastle overloaded with galleries and bartizans, these craft forecast the general lines of the sailing vessel. The dimensions and basic design of the sailing ship changed little during its long history although numerous innovations greatly improved its sailing qualities. From an overall length of 157 feet and beam width of 48 feet in 1698, the proportions of the sailing ship increased to a length of 205 feet and width of 53 feet in 1786, and by 1847, 210 feet by 56 feet. The early seventeenth century saw five classes of sailing ship being produced with twenty-four different gun dispositions. By 1786 only three types of vessels were being constructed and the gunnery arrangements had become standardized.

THE MASTS AND SAILS – AND DEPENDENCE ON THE WEATHER

Early seventeenth-century ships were generally rigged with three masts, the foremast place forward, the mainmast amidships and the mizzen-mast placed towards the stern. The bowsprit projected upwards and outwards from the bows. Masts were made from pine and were crossed by yards which were usually made from fir. Each mast was made up of three sections: the lower mast, the topmast and the topgallant-mast, the sections were joined together at the top and the topmast-trestle-trees. The top was a platform, it was originally circular but later became semicircular with the straight side facing aft built round the lower cross-trees at the point where the topmast was fitted into the lower mast-cap.

Very few changes were made to masts apart from the constant endeavour to strengthen the mast-caps which were never totally satisfactory joints. Masts were lengthened to allow for increased sail area, and in the eighteenth century the mast-head was also lengthened to increase purchase and to strengthen the mast against the violence of the wind. In this way massive structures often resulted with the truck of the mainmast towering 200 feet or more above the water.

In the seventeenth century each mast carried a set of sails comprising three sails, one above the other, the lower, the upper sail and the topgallant sail. On the mainmast, the lower sail was the mainsail, on the foremast it was called the headsail or foresail. The topmast sails were usually known as topsails. Topsails and topgallant sails were known as main topsails, and the mainmast and fore-topsails on the foremast.

A dominating factor in the age of sail was the uncertainty of travel. It was impossible to arrange a sailing time in advance because ships were obliged to a favourable wind in order to clear port and delays would often run into weeks. The duration of a voyage and the date a ship would reach its destination were equally difficult to forecast. A crossing from Europe to the West Indies could take from thirty-five to sixty days, or even longer. Toulon to Gibraltar could be as little as three or four days with a fair wind but it could also take three weeks as the calms in some regions lasted for long periods. Storms frequently blew ships off course and this lengthened the voyage considerably.

With so many uncertainties, a sea voyage before the nineteenth century was an arduous enterprise for both passengers and crew.

Passenger accommodation on board was always very cramped and frequently dirty.

Work demands on the crew varied largely according to the state of the weather. With a settled steady wind the sails needed little trimming and the alterations to sails necessary because of the changes in course could be made from the deck and the tops. When storms blew up and sails needed to be reduced, the crew had to clamber up the masts and along the foot-ropes stretched below the yards to take in the sails. Such manoeuvres required great agility and strength on the part of the sailors as the wind and rain stiffened the canvas and extreme care and sure-footedness were vital.

THE CLIPPER SHIPS

Between 1820 and 1860 the finely-designed, fast clipper ship of the China tea trade was developed which gradually took the place of the heavily built slow sailing ship of the type previously used in the East Indies. Never during the 4,000-year evolution of the sailing-ship did equivalent advances in hull and rig design take place in so short a time.

All praise must go to the master shipwright and his skilled craftsmen who, working with tools which had changed little over the centuries, built the great warships, merchantmen and, finally, the beautiful and highly seaworthy clippers.

In the early nineteenth century, the British East India Company used ships of between 1,200 and 1,500 tons burden for voyages to India and China. These ships were the finest and largest merchant ships of the period.

From its foundation in the seventeenth century and until 1813, the honorable East India Company held a complete monopoly on British trade to the East. Even when the monopoly was abolished the Company still controlled most of the trade until its activities ceased entirely in 1834. Many of the Company's ships were built at dockyards on the River Thames but occasionally shipbuilders at other ports were commissioned and several strong and long-lasting Indiamen were built, largely of tea, at Bombay and Calcutta. One of these, the *Herefordshire,* was built at Bombay in 1813. She was of 1,342 tons burden and was armed with 26 guns. A typical Thames-built Indiaman would have been of about 1,200 tons, 165 feet long, with a beam of 42 feet and a depth of hold of 17 feet.

Because of the great demand for new warships by the Royal Navy during the Napoleonic Wars, there was a shortage of English-grown oak suitable for ship construction. In particularly short supply was the naturally curved wood used for making the angled 'knees' which supported and strengthened the deck beams, and the 'breast-hook', curved struts used in the bows. The Royal Navy had first call on all timber, and the builders of the East India Company's ships had to look to alternative material for certain sections. The Surveyor to the Company proposed that iron 'knees' and 'breast-hooks' be used and this suggestion was adopted by the Company shortly after 1800. Also at this time, the East Indiamen were improved by closing the waist, the space between the quarter-deck, to form a continuous flush upper deck from bow to stern. This innovation was not adopted by the Royal Navy until

The *Wolf,* a brig of war, making signal and laying-to for a pilot off Dover shortly after being taken out of commission by the Royal Navy in the early nineteenth century. Dover Castle can be seen in the background to the right.

The *Macquarie,* a steel-hulled sailing ship of the late nineteenth century, here proudly displays her full sail. A majestic vessel which saw service up until the outbreak of the First World War.

the 1830s.

To provide maximum cargo-carrying capacity the Indiaman was designed with a full body and flat floors, the extreme sloping inwards or tumble-home of the upper works of the eighteenth-century East Indiaman were greatly reduced. The round bow was built right up to the level of the forecastle deck, and at the stern and quarters two tiers of windows, without projecting galleries, allowed daylight into the large cabins. The deck below the upper deck was known in an Indiaman as the middle deck, here the main defensive armaments of about twenty-six 18-pounder guns were carried. Below the middle deck was the lower deck, this was used for cargo stowage and did not usually carry guns and was infrequently fitted with gunports, but to make it appear that the ship carried a heavy armament many Indiamen had a line of dummy ports painted at lower-deck level. Contemporary records show that on occasion the large East Indiamen were mistaken for 64-gun warships. These merchant ships were all ship-rigged – three-masted with square sails on all masts and a fore-and-aft gaff mizzen-sail. Numerous staysails were also set between the masts and between the foremasts and bowsprit. In suitable wind conditions studding-sails – small sails set at the sides of the square-sails – and other extra sails were used. The East Indiaman *Essex* is said to have hoisted a total of sixty-three sails on occasion. The crew of an East Indiaman was organised and disciplined in the same manner as the crew of a warship, but with a much smaller armament fewer men were needed. An Indiaman of about 1,200 tons carried a complement of some 130 men including the commander, six mates, surgeon, purser, midshipman, gunners, boatswain, carpenter, caulker sail-maker and cook.

With the advent of the first transatlantic steamship service in 1838, *and* a steamship service from the Red Sea to India in 1840, it became clear that larger and much faster sailing ships would be needed to compete with the growing threat of steam.

Between the years 1837 and 1841, Green and Wigram, the shipbuilders and owners, launched eight vessels of a new type, ranging in size from the *Madagascar* of a little over 800 tons to the *Southampton* of nearly 1,000 tons. In 1842, with the launch from the same yard of the *Prince of Wales* of 1,200 tons, the new design was extended to the largest ships. The *Prince of Wales* was 179 feet long and 39 feet wide showing an advance in length-to-breadth ratio of about 4.3 to 1 compared to the 4 to 1 proportions of the last East Indiamen. The *Prince of Wales'* long flush deck was to become the distinctive mark of the Blackwall frigates, closely resembling in appearance a 50-gun frigate of the period.

In 1843 the partnership between Green and Wigram was dissolved and the shipyard divided into two separate ports. The now quite separate companies of M. Wigram & Sons and R. & H. Green continued to build and operate large, well-designed ships.

Ships of the Blackwall-frigate type continued to be built on the Thames, and in the north of England at Sunderland and on the River Tyne. The northern-built vessels are classified as Blackwall frigates. Two particularly fine vessels, the *Marlborough* and the *Blenheim* were built at T. & W. Smith's yard on the Tyne. Both vessels won awards at the Great Exhibition of 1851 in London, and were considered to be the finest ships in the British mercantile

From left to right: a fishing smack, a schooner and a sloop-rigged barge. Such views were common on the coast and estuaries in the early nineteenth century when the economy of the country was so much more dependent on water transportation.

fleet. The *Marlborough,* built in 1846 was of 1,402 tons, 1,975 feet long and 41 feet wide. The *Blenheim* was built in 1848 and was a slightly smaller ship of 1,314 tons. Both vessels had flush decks and were without a raised poop or deck-house at the stern.

The need to build faster sailing ships led to a good deal of experiment with hull shape and design. In Scotland, James and William Hall of the Aberdeen shipbuilding company Alexander Hall & Sons, used a water tank to test scale models, and in 1839 built a schooner, the *Scottish Maid,* which proved a very fast vessel and was considered by some to be the first clipper ship. The *Scottish Maid,* of 142 tons, was 92 feet long, with a beam of 19 feet, and was designed with 'a sharpening of the bow by carrying out the stem to the cutwater'. This form of bow became known as the Aberdeen Bow. The *Scottish Maid* was employed on the Aberdeen–London service and is said to have frequently made the journey in forty-nine hours. Other schooners were built to the same design and proved even more successful.

Following the repeal of the British Navigation Acts in 1849, British ports were opened to ships of all nations, and this coincided with a great increase in demand for tea in Britain which led, not surprisingly, to American clippers being used to carry tea to London. The *Oriental,* of 1,003 tons, was the first American tea clipper to unload her cargo in London, in December 1850.

With British companies either chartering or buying American ships, British yards worked even harder to produce fast, competitive clippers. In 1850, Alexander Hall & Sons, already famous for their fast schooners, built a small clipper, *Stornoway.* The following year this vessel made an outward journey to China

via India, returning from Whampoa to London in 104 days. The *Stornoway* was of 595 registered tons, 157 feet long and with a beam of 25 feet. In 1851 the same company built the *Chrysolite,* of similar dimensions to the *Stornoway* she proved a fast and highly successful vessel continuing in the China trade for nearly fifteen years. In 1852 the Thames yard of R. & H. Green, already well known for their Blackwall frigates, built the clipper *Challenger.* This ship is recorded as having made the outward journey to China in the then relatively short time of 101 days.

By the mid-1850s numerous British shipyards were building clippers, and many fine vessels were produced for the China and Australia services by shipbuilders on the Clyde, in Sunderland and in Liverpool.

The difficulties of securing suitable supplies of hardwood, allied to the obvious costructional advantages of iron-built ships, brought about a form of construction known as composite building. In such ships the interior framework and other supports were of iron, with the external planking of wood which would be sheathed in copper below the water-line.

Three ships built by the Liverpool shipbuilders Henry Jordan and John Getty serve to illustrate the development of the composite-built ship. In July 1850 a small 33-ton, 50-feet schooner called the *Excelsior* was launched by the yard. This was followed in 1851 by a three-masted barque-rigged vessel, the *Marion Macintyre,* of 283 tons and 115 feet length. The third vessel, the *Tubal Cain,* also launched in 1851, was a ship-rigged vessel of 788 tons, with two decks and a length of 115 feet.

Perhaps the most beautiful clippers to be built by Robert Steele

& Company were the *Ariel* and the *Sir Lancelot.* Both ships were launched in 1865. The *Ariel,* of 886 tons, had a length of 195 feet, a beam of 33 feet and a depth in hold of 21 feet. The *Sir Lancelot* was of similar dimensions, and apart from certain differences in the arrangement of the deck fittings, the vessels were sister ships. Both were constructed with iron frames, planked with teak and elm, their hulls sheathed in yellow metal with the lower masts of iron.

The last years of the 1860s saw the construction of two composite clippers about which more has been written than on any other ship of the type. In August 1868 the *Thermopylae* was launched. She was designed by a successful naval architect, Bernard Waymouth, and built by Walter Hood of Aberdeen. The vessel was 212 feet long with a beam of 36 feet, a depth of 20 feet, and a ranking stem and rounded fore-foot. A deep false keel gave more grip on the water and assisted the ship when sailing windward. The *Thermopylae* was painted green with white lower masts and yards. The sail plan was of particular interest in that the emphasis was on width rather than height, the main yard was 80 feet long. The *Thermopylae* was built for the Aberdeen White Star Line and on her maiden voyage reached Melbourne in sixty-three days from Gravesend, returning to London with a cargo of tea from China. The *Thermopylae* remained in the tea trade until 1881, and in 1890 she was sold to a Canadian company and was used to carry rice from the East across the Pacific. In 1895 she was bought by the Portuguese Government, converted into a training ship and renamed the *Pedro Nunes.* The end of this great ship came twelve years later, when she was towed out to sea and sunk with full naval honours off the mouth of the Tagus.

The *Cutty Sark* is perhaps even better known than the *Thermopylae.* The two ships were rivals, and indeed *Cutty Sark* was built as a direct competitor to *Thermopylae.* The former was designed by a then little-known naval architect, Hercules Linton, and built at the Dumbarton yard of Scott & Linton. The contract price for the ship was to be no more than £16,150 and only the best materials and work were to be employed. Trying to adhere to the contract bankrupted Scott & Linton, and the ship had to be finished by the neighbouring firm of Denny Bros.

Hercules Linton had succeeded in designing a clipper which incorporated the best features of other successful vessels. The bows were extremely sharp, the midship section was full with square bilges, a fine underwater body at the stern with a pronounced counter and an almost right angle fore-foot gave the *Cutty Sark* great speed through the water – she is recorded to have sailed at $17\frac{1}{2}$ knots on one occasion, and made a day's run of 363 miles. The ship had excellent qualities when sailing windward. The *Cutty Sark* with a length of 212 feet, a beam of 36 feet and a depth of hold of 21 feet was six inches longer than the *Thermpoylae* but her tonnage was 963 gross compared with the 991 tons of the latter.

The *Cutty Sark* was launched in November 1869 and intended for the China tea trade. Exactly one week earlier, on 16 November 1869, the Suez Canal was opened, thus making a shorter sea route, via the Mediterranean, available to steamers while the sailing ships were still forced to voyage by way of the Cape of Good Hope. By 1880 with no more tea cargoes to be had the *Cutty Sark* began carrying wool, and it was during this period that she made some of her fastest times. In 1887–8 she made the

19

The three-masted *Thetis*, a West Indiaman, preparing for a voyage off the coast of the Isle of Wight in 1822. Note the sleek lines of this typical cargo vessel designed for traversing the Atlantic.

record time of seventy-one days from Sydney to London. In that same season the *Thermopylae* completed the journey in seventy-nine days. Between the years 1888 and 1895 all of the *Cutty Sark's* Australian voyages, both outward and homeward, were completed in under 100 days. In the period of the tea trade the clippers raced to reach London with the new season's crop, the first thereby commanding the highest prices. Now that the clippers carried wool, speed was just as important and there were good profits to be made. The slowest ships were loaded first so that they would reach London in time for the January and February wool sales, while the *Cutty Sark* and other fast ships were kept back for late loading, the captains being sufficiently confident in their ability to make up for lost time. It was as a wool clipper that the *Cutty Sark* came into her own, outsailing all her rivals including the great *Thermopylae*.

In 1895 the *Cutty Sark* was sold to the Portuguese brothers Ferreira who changed her name to their own, and as the *Ferreira* of Lisbon she continued in service for the next twenty-six years. She was re-rigged as a three-masted barquentine in 1916 after being overhauled. In 1922 she was sold to another Portuguese company who renamed her *Maria do Amparo*. A few months later she was sold yet again, this time to Captain Dowman who reconditioned, restored and re-rigged her. *Cutty Sark* remained at Falmouth until 1938 when she was presented to the Thames Nautical Training College. In 1953 the vessel was taken over by the *Cutty Sark* Preservation Society, and on 10 December 1954 she was moved into a specially constructed dry-dock at Greenwich where, as the only surviving example of a tea clipper, she remains to this day a national monument.

The *Torrens*, built by James Laing at Sunderland and launched in 1875, was one of the last large composite sailing vessels to be built. She was designed specially for the passenger trade to Australia, and was managed by the Elder Line. The *Torrens*, weighing some 1,276 tons, was 222 feet long with a beam of 38 feet and a depth in hold of 21 feet.

Joseph Conrad, the novelist served as second mate on the *Torrens* for two years from November 1891. He described the vessel as 'a ship of brilliant qualities', a fine tribute from one of the few writers who really did understand the sea's attraction for all of humankind.

SAILING SHIPS IN STEEL

During the 1870s good quality mild steel became available to British shipbuilders, and by using mild steel to replace iron plates the weight of a ship could be reduced by some fifteen per cent. The substitution of steel for iron led also to a general increase in the size of sailing ships, and after 1890 some huge square-rigged vessels of over 5,000 tons were built.

Between the years 1888 and 1894 a large number of sailing ships were built. These vessels were designed to carry cargo and not for speed, they carried small crews and numerous mechanical aids, enabling them to compete with the steam 'tramp ship'. Because of their all-important role of cargo carriers, these steel ships were built with full midship sections and sharp bilges with nearly flat floors. They were contemptuously described by some as 'steel

Looking more like a fantasia by a latter-day Piranesi, this prison ship of the early 1800s presents a spectacle more ignominious for a vessel than being sunk by the enemy. The three 'gaols' which have been built on the main deck conspire to present the view of a floating shanty-town.

boxes', but in fact many of the sailing ships built in the 1890s had fine sailing qualities and even when heavily laden could make good time. On occasion their mean effective speed over long ocean voyages was only a few knots slower than the celebrated clippers. The most commonly used rig at this period was the three- and four-masted barque rig.

As sailing ships increased in length, modifications were made to the deck layout. Flying gangways or bridges were constructed to connect the poop and forecastle by way of the roofs of the deck-houses, making it easier for the crew to move about the ship in heavy weather. In about 1884, a midship structure known as a bridge deck was introduced on larger ships. This bridge deck extended across the width of the vessel, giving the hull increased longitudinal strength and also providing good accommodation for the crew and a safe, centrally placed position from which the vessel could be controlled.

And so, as the nineteenth century drew to a close the day of the great sailing ship was virtually over. Demands on materials were matched by the need to introduce faster and more commodious vessels. The steamship inevitably gained swift acceptance for both commercial and military purposes.

As the age of steam came in, the majestic sailing ships diminished in number, until, by the 1930s there were few left anywhere. In Britain today only half a dozen remain: one of them, Nelson's three-decker warship the *Victory,* and another, the *Cutty Sark,* probably the most famous clipper ship of all. A mute testimony to the days when manpower was as essential for a day's sailing as the very wind itself.

H.M.S. Pomone off the coast of Ireland in the early 1800s. She was a 38-gun frigate launched in 1803 and saw little action prior to being lost off the Needles in 1811.

THE PLATES

A Ship of Henry V

This type of ship was in general use at the time of the Battle of Agincourt in 1415. Its most noticeable features were the high forecastle and high stern gallery; these enabled the bowmen to shoot down into the lower decks of the enemy ships. (It has to be remembered that at this date the heavy gun had not been developed for use at sea, consequently the sides were not pierced with gunports.)

The 'Great Age of Discovery' had not yet begun, so these ships were used primarily to transport Henry's armies across the Channel and, secondly, as merchantmen carrying goods and personnel to and from the Continent. Because the beam was half the length they were inclined to be unwieldy in heavy weather.

Towards the end of the fifteenth century all ships became armed and there were no merchantmen as such. This meant that all vessels were designed to serve in battle and as cargo carriers.

Cargoes, at this time, consisted of woollens, skins and light goods. Later, as ships became bigger, voyages longer, and home consumptions increased, much heavier consignments of grain, timber and iron ores were carried.

PLATE I

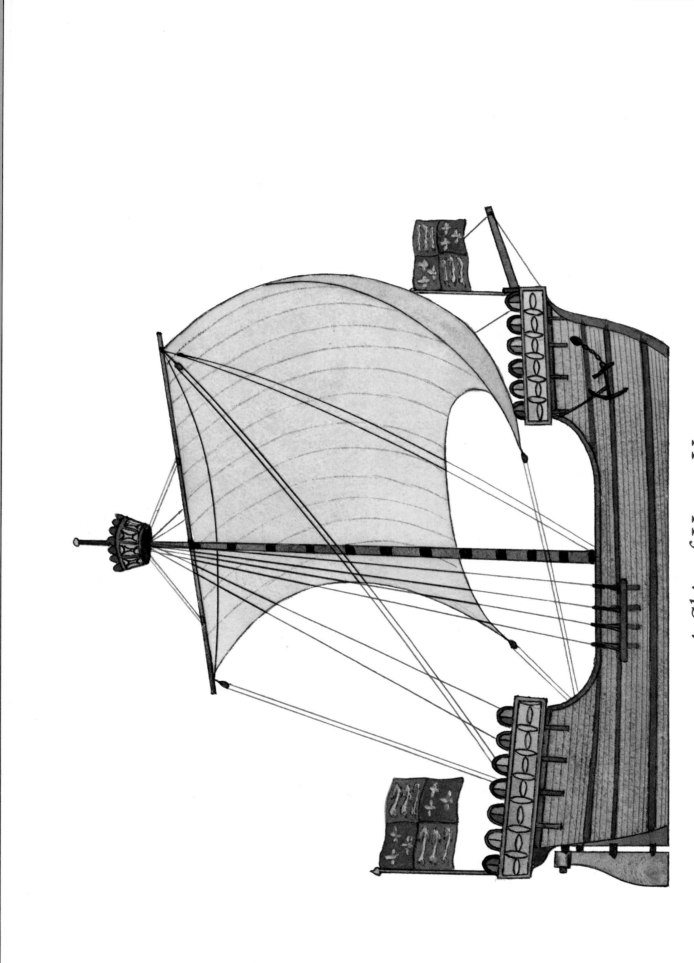

A Ship of Henry V

The Henry Grace à Dieu

Henry Grace à Dieu – better known as the *Great Harry* – was built by Henry VIII in 1514 to meet the ever threatening menace of Spain. She was the pride of Henry's navy and the follow-on to one of his earlier ships, the *Regent*, which had been lost through fire.

The largest ship to be built by Henry, the *Great Harry* weighed 1,500 tons and was more like a fortress than a ship. She had 130 medium-sized cannon, as well as 21 bronze cannon; including her lighter armament, she carried a total of 184 guns. (Some of these were added later after rebuilding.)

Soldiers were regarded as almost more important than sailors on the *Great Harry* and, together, soldiers, sailors and gunners totalled 800 men.

Despite the fact the *Great Harry* was the most powerful and advanced ship of her time, she had many faults. Fitted with four towering masts, she was top-heavy and when in full canvas was sometimes more dangerous to herself than the enemy. Her overall weight had to be reduced to ensure correct sailing; it was cut from 1,500 tons to 1,000 tons.

Sadly, the *Great Harry* never had a chance to prove herself in battle, for she suffered the fate of many of her kind in this period – she was destroyed by fire, at Woolwich in 1553.

PLATE II

The Henry Grace à Dieu

The Ark Royal

The *Ark Royal* was built in 1546, during the reign of Queen Elizabeth I, to the design of Sir Walter Raleigh, but was bought from him for the State. She was the first ship in the British Navy to bear the name *Ark Royal*, and all ships so named subsequently had illustrious careers.

She was typical of the Elizabethan galleons of the period and performed well in service and battle – particularly in the battle of the Spanish Armada, in 1588, which earnt her a place in history.

Weighing 800 tons, the *Ark Royal* carried a crew of 430 men, made up of soldiers and gunners as well as sailors. In battle, the main armament of this type of ship consisted of about 20 large muzzle-loading guns and a range of smaller cannon. Records of the period show that due to the varying calibres of weapons, it was almost impossible to carry a sufficient supply of different kinds of shot that could sustain a long engagement; and it was said that when in battle with ships of the Spanish Armada, many English ships had to withdraw owing to lack of ammunition. England's victory, however, undercut any truth there might have been in the argument.

In 1608, under King James I, the ship was renamed *Ann Royal*.

PLATE III

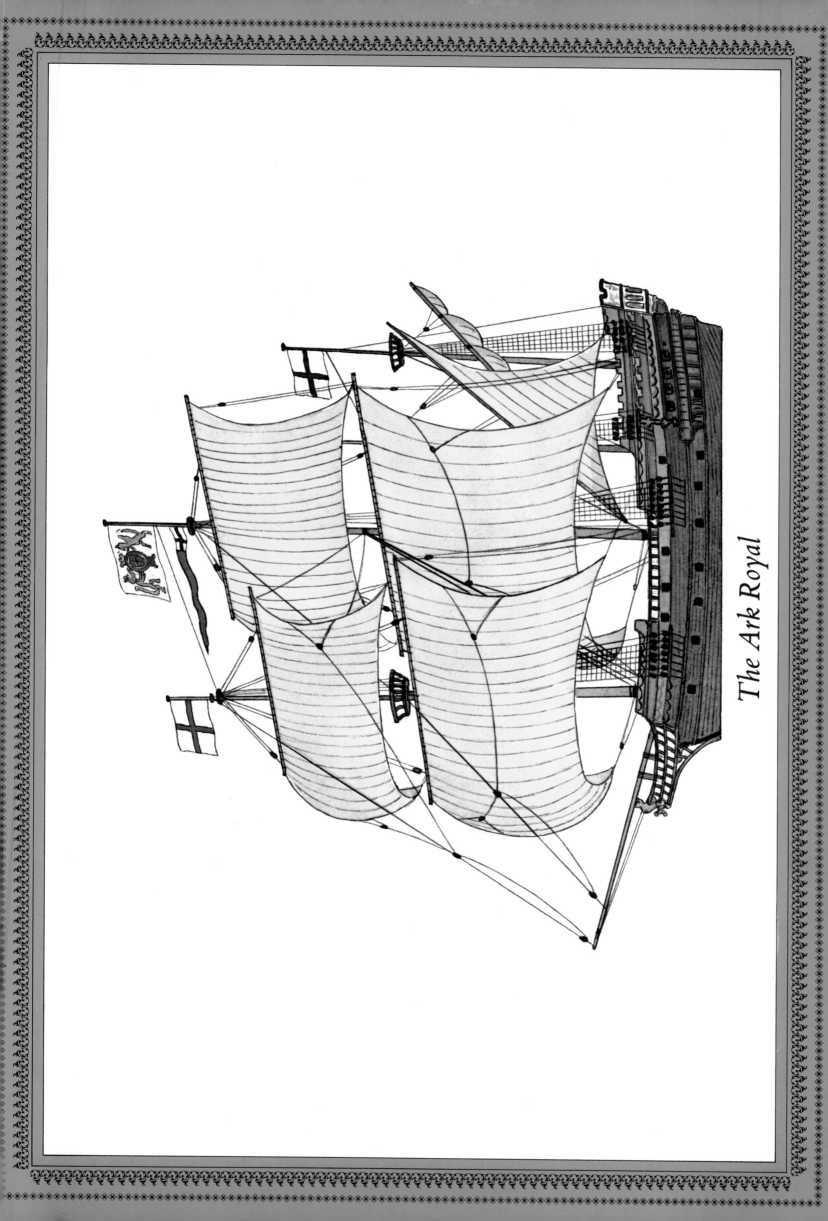

The Ark Royal

The Mayflower

The *Mayflower* will for ever be remembered as the ship that carried the Pilgrim Fathers to America in pursuit of a new life in the New World. She was square-rigged, with an overall length of 90 feet, a keel length of 64 feet, and a hold depth of 11 feet.

In consort with the *Speedwell*, the *Mayflower* sailed originally from Southampton on 15 August 1620. They encountered severe storms in the English Channel, however, and *Speedwell* was badly damaged. Both ships returned to Plymouth and after refitting, *Mayflower* sailed alone on 16 September. She carried 101 crew and passengers; of these, sixty-six were English and thirty-five from Leyden, Holland. Their aim was to set up the first permanent colony in America.

The Pilgrims' journey lasted sixty-six days, during which time they encountered much bad weather. With most of the passengers in a state of severe sickness, a landing was finally made in November, and a colony established at Plymouth, Massachusetts. By the winter of that year, however, half of the original company of passengers had died from illness.

PLATE IV

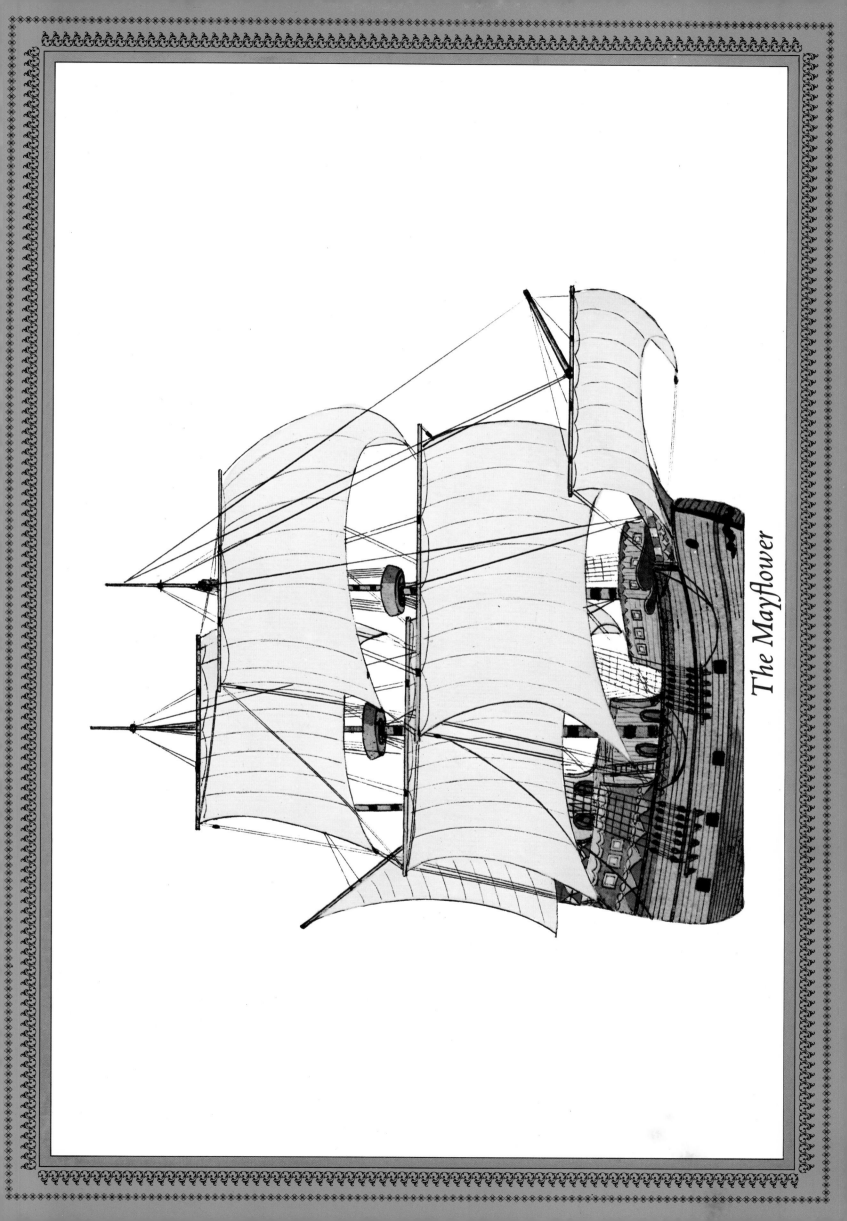

The Mayflower

The Royal Charles

The *Royal Charles* was one of the first three-deckers built and, together with the *Royal Prince*, formed part of the navy of James I during the early part of the seventeenth century. The ship had a keel length of almost 130 feet and a beam length of 45 feet. Prior to the Third Dutch War she underwent a complete refit.

The *Royal Charles* carried some 50 guns, and during the wars with the Dutch was one of the main contestants in battle. On 1 June 1666 the Four Days Battle commenced in the narrows of the English Channel. The engagement lasted four days with varying fortunes and inconclusive results. The *Royal Charles* was the flagship of the Duke of Albemarle, and he decided to attack.

One of the Dutch, De Witt, said afterwards, 'if the English are beaten, their defeat did them more honour than their former victories. All the Dutch had discovered was that Englishmen might be killed and English ships burnt, but that English courage was invincible.'

The *Royal Charles* ran aground in this battle, as did the *Royal Prince*, but the *Royal Charles* was successfully refloated and remained in action until the battle was over. The *Royal Prince*, however, had to be burnt to prevent recapture.

PLATE V

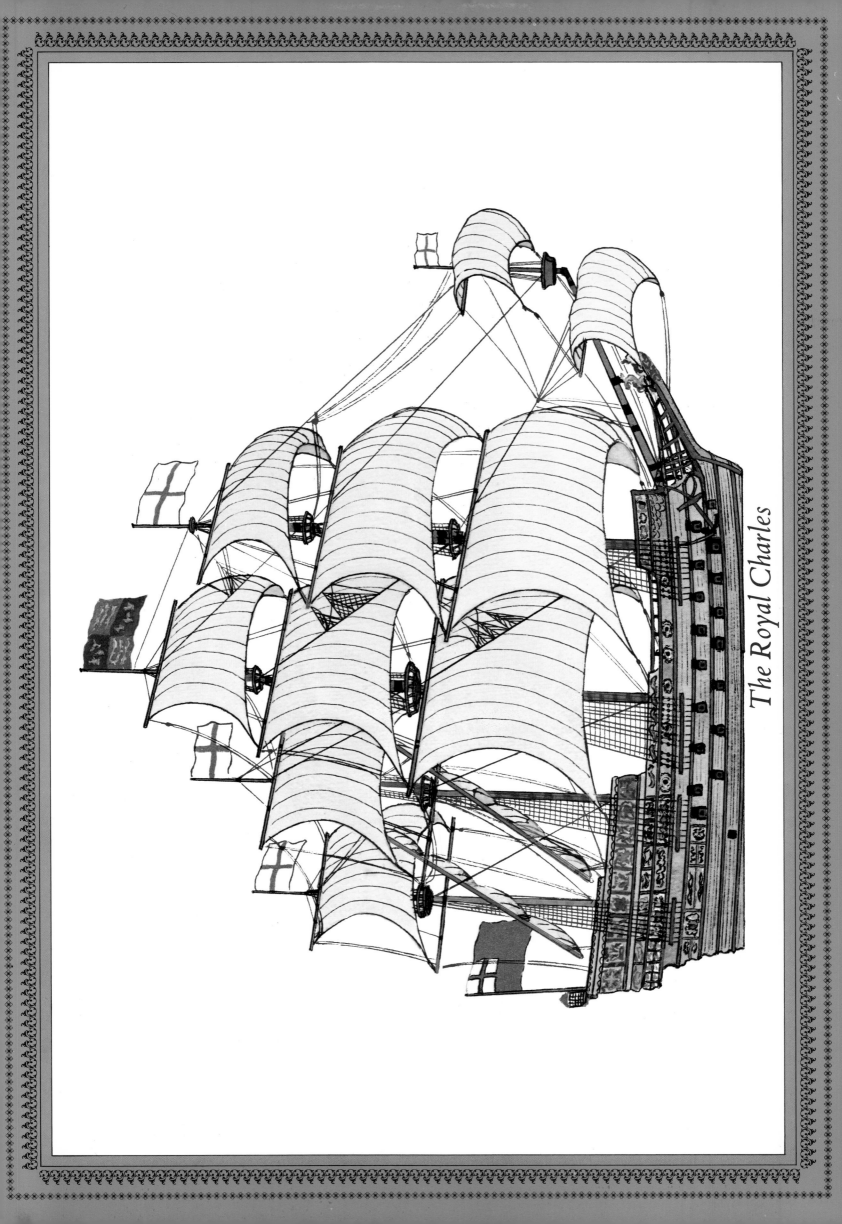

The Royal Charles

The Centurion

The *Centurion* was a 64-gun two-decker and was commanded by Commodore George Anson in a glorious career prior to Trafalgar. In 1743 she captured the Spanish vessel *Covadonga*, which was carrying a shipment of gold, and in 1747 she was part of an English naval force under Anson (who was now Admiral) that attacked a French convoy bound for Canada. Some of the convoy escaped, but one French frigate was sunk and four merchant ships were captured and sent to England with prize crews in possession.

The *Centurion* was typical of her class as a third rate, with a main armament of 32-pounder guns and a secondary armament of lighter weapons carried on the main deck. Ship design had stabilized somewhat by this time, with emphasis being placed upon more efficient rigging.

English weapons and gunnery during this period were regarded generally as the finest in the world, and other foreign powers tried to emulate them. Ships like the *Centurion* laid the foundations for the much more powerful British Navy which was to follow.

PLATE VI

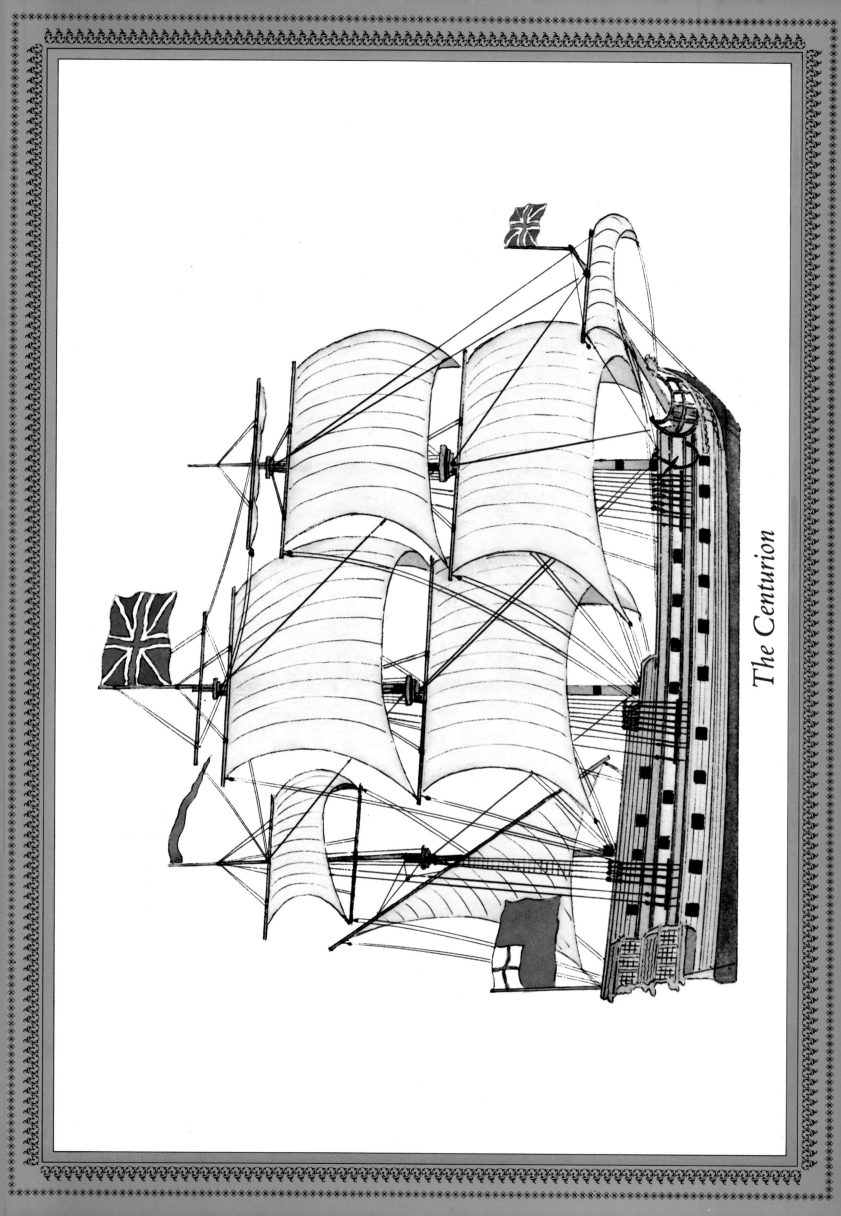

The Centurion

The Torbay

The *Torbay*, originally named *Neptune*, was built at Deptford in 1683 as a second rate, 99-gun ship. Weighing 1,475 tons, she had a length of 124 feet, a beam of 41 feet and a draught of 20 feet. Her peacetime complement of men was 500, but this was increased to 660 men in periods of war. In 1750 the ship was refitted and converted to a third rate 74-gun ship and the original upper gundeck was removed.

In 1759 the *Torbay* served as Admiral Keppel's flagship. In the Battle of Quiberon Bay, which took place off the French coast near Brest, she fought with distinction and inflicted heavy losses on the French fleet. The French fleet consisted of twenty men-of-war, two frigates and two corvettes while the British fleet consisted of twenty-three men-of-war.

When the French realized their severe opposition, they endeavoured to retreat between two rocks known as The Cardinals. But superb seamanship on the part of Admiral Hawke took advantage of the French act and trapped them between the rocks and the guns of the British fleet. *Torbay* emerged damaged but victorious.

PLATE VII

The Torbay

The Warren Hastings

The British East India Company was formed by Royal Charter in 1600 and lasted until 1834, when the charter was rescinded. In 1808, when the company was at its peak, it was operating fifty-four ships (totalling more than 45,000 tons) between London, India and China. These East Indiamen – as they were called – left England carrying cargoes of household goods, wines and watches; they returned laden with spices, sugar, ivory and more often than not, opium. The officers of this fleet were said to be the élite of the shipping world.

At this time all merchant ships were armed and could be regarded as worthy opponents for contemporary warships of similar size, and more than a match for privateers of the period.

The *Warren Hastings* was one of these East Indiamen, but was less fortunate than some in battle. While on her way home from China to Portsmouth in 1805, she was attacked by the French naval frigate *Piemontaise*, and after a battle lasting five hours the *Warren Hastings* was defeated by the superior-gunned French frigate and towed away as a prize capture.

PLATE VIII

The Warren Hastings

H.M.S. Agamemnon

Built on the Beaulieu River at Buckler's Yard in 1781, the *Agamemnon* was a 64-gun, two-decker ship on the line, and a strong addition to England's navy.

Her hull was sheathed in 30 tons of copper, and almost 100 tons of wrought iron were used in the internal structure. This large quantity of metal was due, in part, to the increasing shortage of timber at this time. Her constructon took just over eighteen months – quite an achievement in an age when few mechanical aids to building were available.

Agamemnon served actively in the Mediterranean and was said to have been the favourite command of Lord Nelson.

PLATE IX

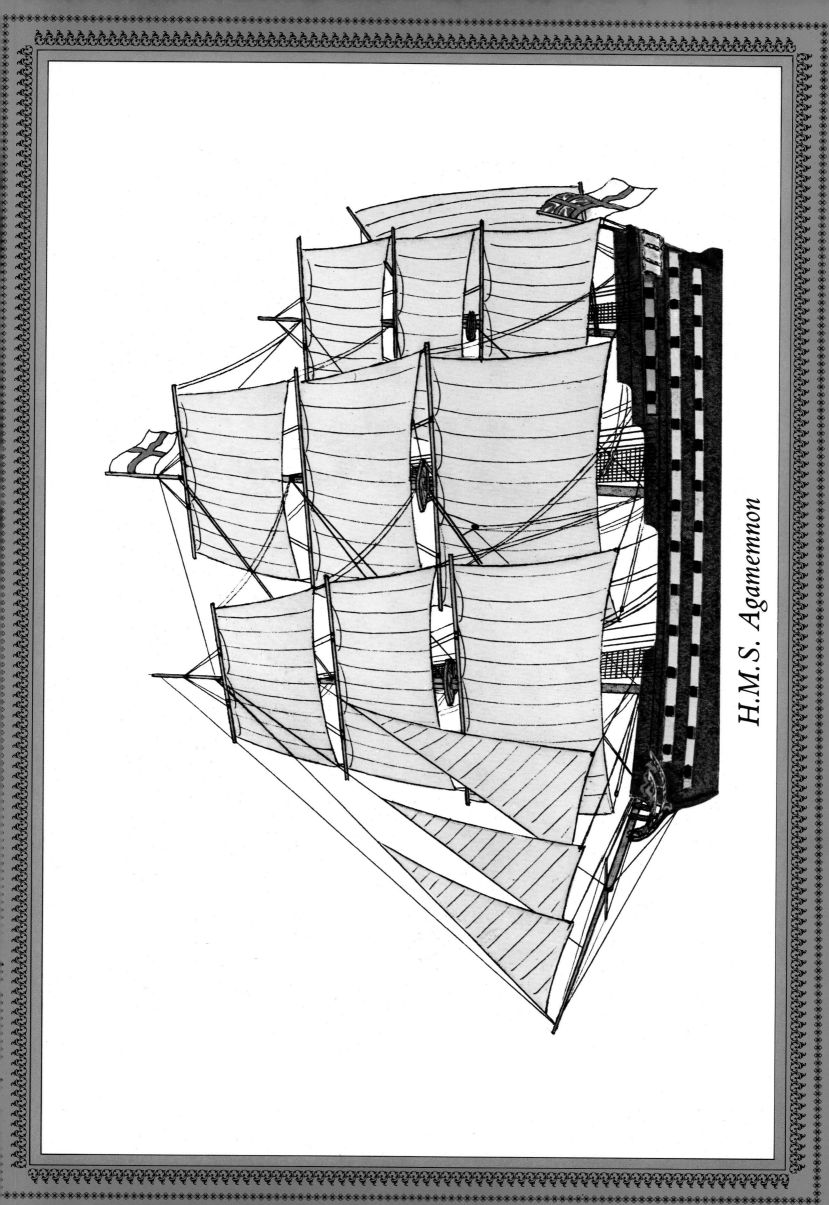

H.M.S. Agamemnon

74-gun Ship

Between 1760 and 1820 there was a large number of 74-gun ships in commission classified as third rates; a fine example of which would have been the *Illustrious*, built in 1803. Her gundeck length was 175 feet.

These ships had two main gundecks and weighed between 1,650 and 1,700 tons. Their main armament consisted of carriage-mounted 32-pounder guns; and a secondary armament was made up of various carronades and half-pounder rail-mounted weapons. The total complement of officers and men was about 600.

In spite of missing some of the fame of the first rates, the 74-gun ship was, nevertheless, a most important part of Britain's navy and an excellent fighting ship.

PLATE X

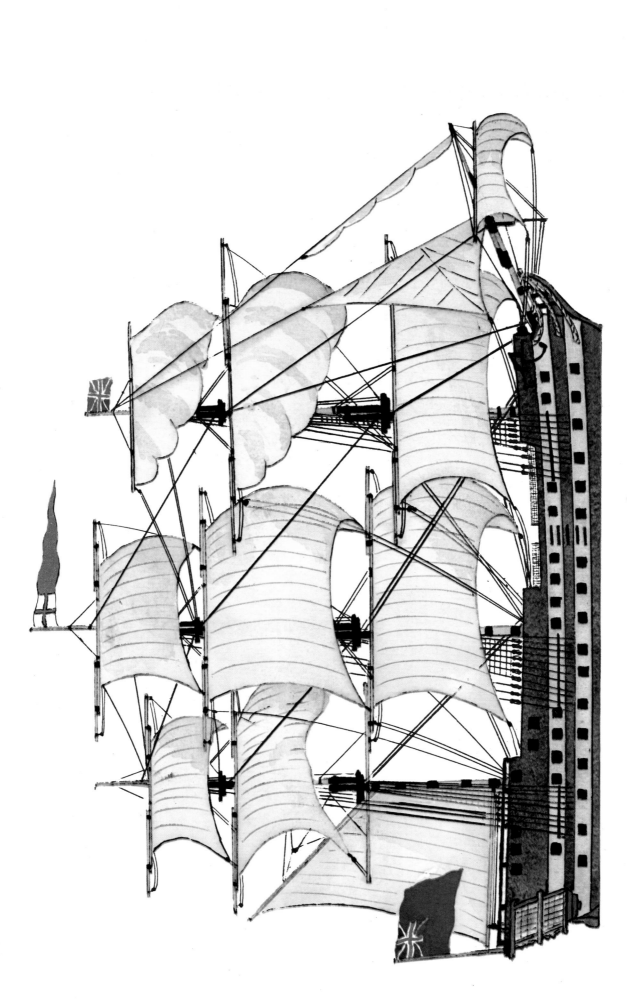

74-gun Ship

H.M.S. *Victory*

Built in the dockyard at Chatham according to an admiralty commission of 1758, the *Victory* was twice rebuilt before the famous Battle of Trafalgar in October 1805.

Weighing 2,163 tons she had a keel length of 150 feet in teak, and a double-layered hull in English oak – the bottom of which was sheathed in copper. The overall length was 226 feet, the beam 52 feet and the height, keel to mast-head, 200 feet. Her armament consisted of 102 guns, with 32-pounders having a range of $1\frac{1}{2}$ miles, 28 24-pounders, 30 12-pounders, and 10 12-pounders on the half-deck. At the forecastle there were 2 12-pounders and 2 68-pound carronades.

The *Victory* was the flagship for the admirals Keppel, Hardy, Kempenfelt, Howe, Hood, and most famous of all, Nelson. She came into the Battle of Trafalgar in October 1805 under the command of Nelson; and it was during this battle with the French that Nelson was fatally shot by a rifleman mounted in the rigging of an enemy ship. The *Victory* was damaged during the fighting and towed to Gibraltar for repairs; she was then sent home for a refit.

After Trafalgar she was used as a flagship for the Port Admiral, Portsmouth and finally in 1848 for the Commander-in-Chief, Portsmouth.

In 1922 it was considered that she should be scrapped. An order to preserve her was gained, however, and she was permanently dry-docked. The *Victory* is one of the few great sailing ships still to be seen, and is now in the Royal Naval dockyard at Portsmouth where she is visited annually by more than 250,000 people.

PLATE XI

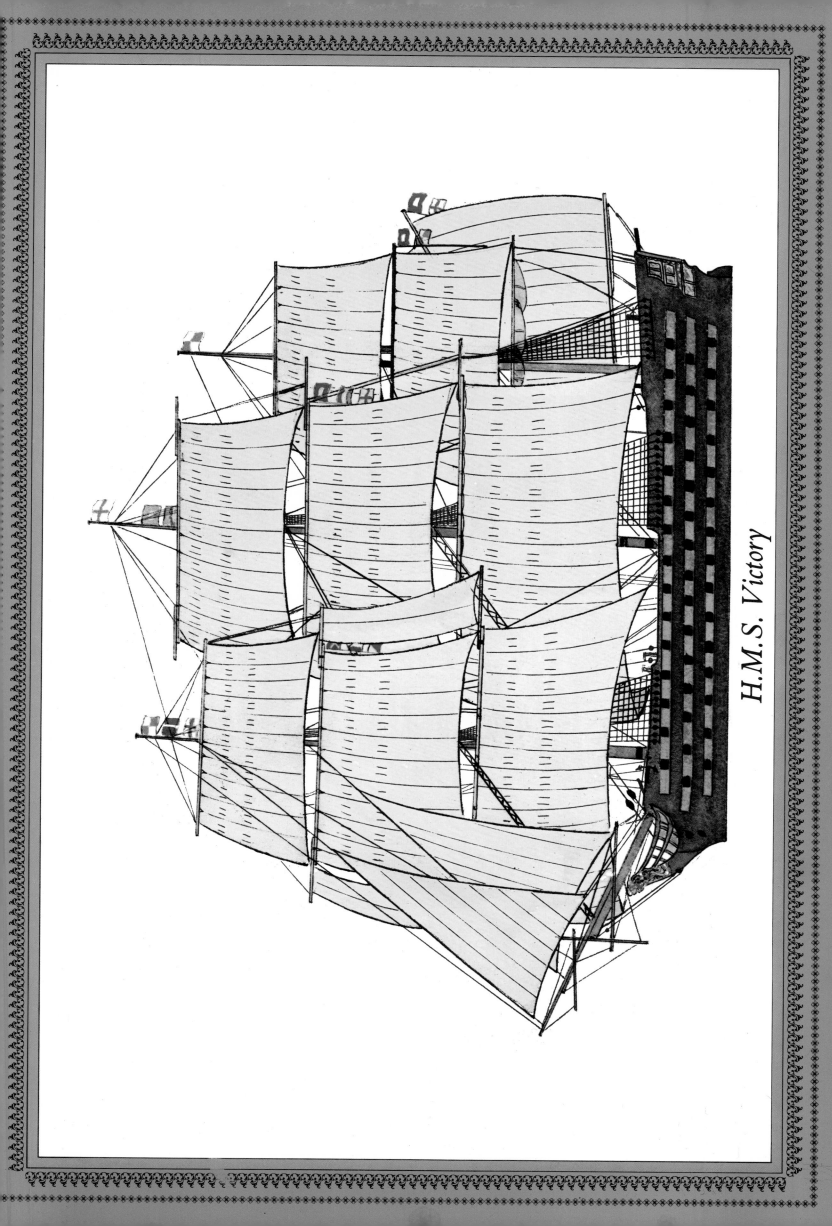

H.M.S. Victory

The Shanon

The *Shanon* was launched at Frindsbury on the Medway in 1806. A frigate of 1,066 tons, her keel length was 150 feet and her beam length 40 feet. Although classified as a 38-gun frigate her armament consisted of 28 18-pounder cannons, 2 9-pounder cannons and 16 32-pounder carronades. The discrepancy in the figures quoted for the number of weapons carried, and her classification as a 38-gun frigate is due to the peculiar rating of ships during this period, which did not include carronades.

Up to 1811 she was under the command of Captain Broke, who had acquired an able and efficient crew while patrolling and blockading the French coast.

.In June 1813 *Shanon* and the frigate *Tenedos* were despatched to America. While lying off Boston, *Shanon* encountered the American frigate *Chesapeake* emerging from the harbour and a short, but furious, battle followed. Both ships were lying hove-to and firing broadsides at each other, and each suffered severe casualties. *Shanon*, however, was victorious and succeeded in capturing the *Chesapeake*, which was then taken into service by the Royal Navy and kept in commission until 1819.

Shanon was based in Halifax, Nova Scotia, until the end of the American war in 1814. She returned to England in 1831 and after further service was broken up at Chatham in 1859.

PLATE XII

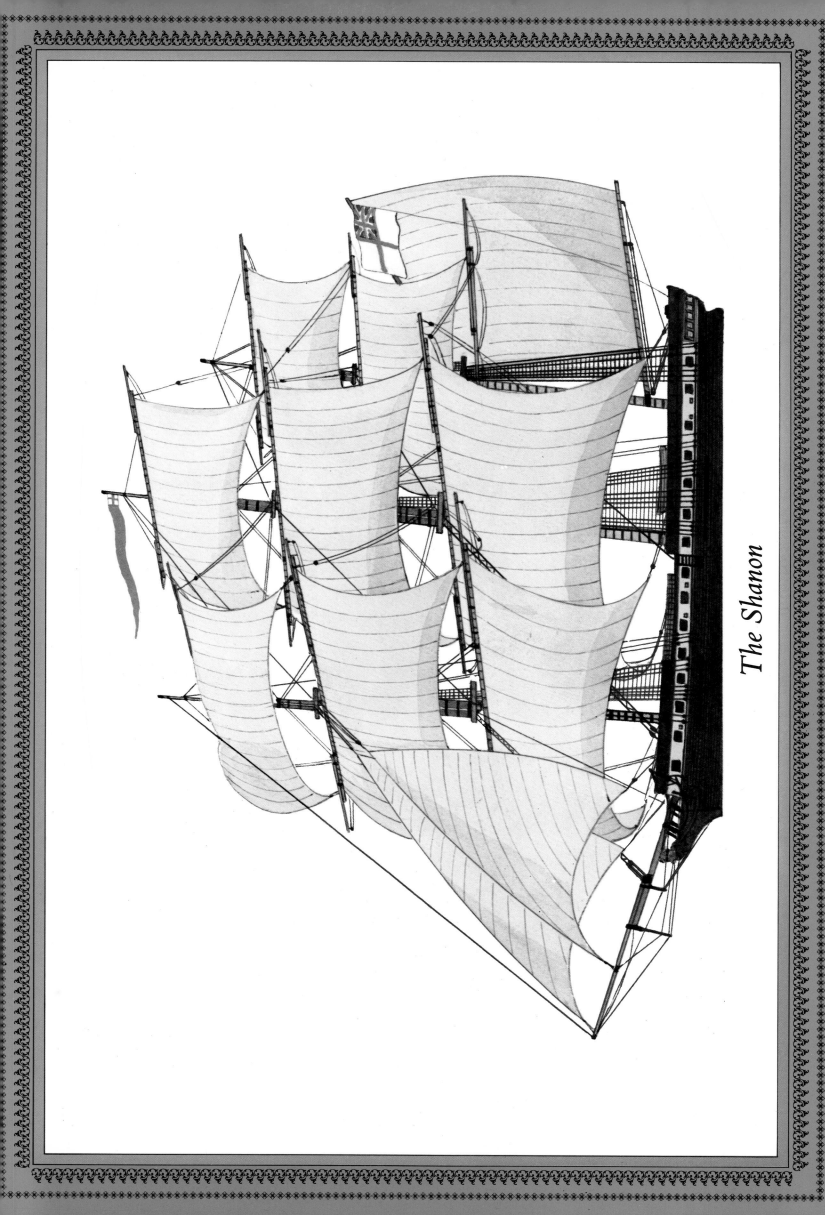

The Shanon

The Java

This 49-gun frigate must be regarded as one of England's finest ships. In December 1812 while on patrol near Bahia, South America, she sighted the 59-gun American ship, *Constitution*: battle ensigns were hoisted by both ships and fighting commenced in the war between England and America.

Although outgunned, *Java* fought gloriously and endeavoured to get close alongside *Constitution* in order to board her. This action unfortunately met with a full broadside from *Constitution*, and *Java* was damaged beyond repair. Although badly wounded, her captain, Captain Bainbridge, directed operations until being finally taken prisoner on the *Constitution* where he died.

The losses on the *Java* amounted to 60 dead and 170 wounded, while *Constitution's* losses were only 9 dead and fewer than 30 wounded.

Java's courage thus earnt her a place in the annals of British naval warfare.

PLATE XIII

The Java

S.S. *Great Britain*

This ship was built in 1845 at Bristol by the famous engineer Isambard Kingdom Brunel, whose dream it was to extend his transport systems to America.

Great Britain was built of iron, and originally had six masts with sails. She was propeller-driven and easily the largest ship of the time.

Her career was varied. In 1846 she ran aground at Dundrum Bay on the Irish Coast, and since her owners could not finance the project further she was sold to some Australians. She was rerigged with five masts, but later converted to a sailing ship with three masts. In 1886 she was used as a coal hulk in the Falkland Islands, where she finished her operational days and remained until 1970.

In 1970 a number of prominent Bristolians thought that due to the still excellent condition of the hull she should be brought back to England and restored to her original form. The hull was towed by means of a floating dry-dock from the Falkland Islands to the original launching place in Bristol. *Great Britain* is now being slowly reconditioned and will ultimately be on display at Bristol.

PLATE XIV

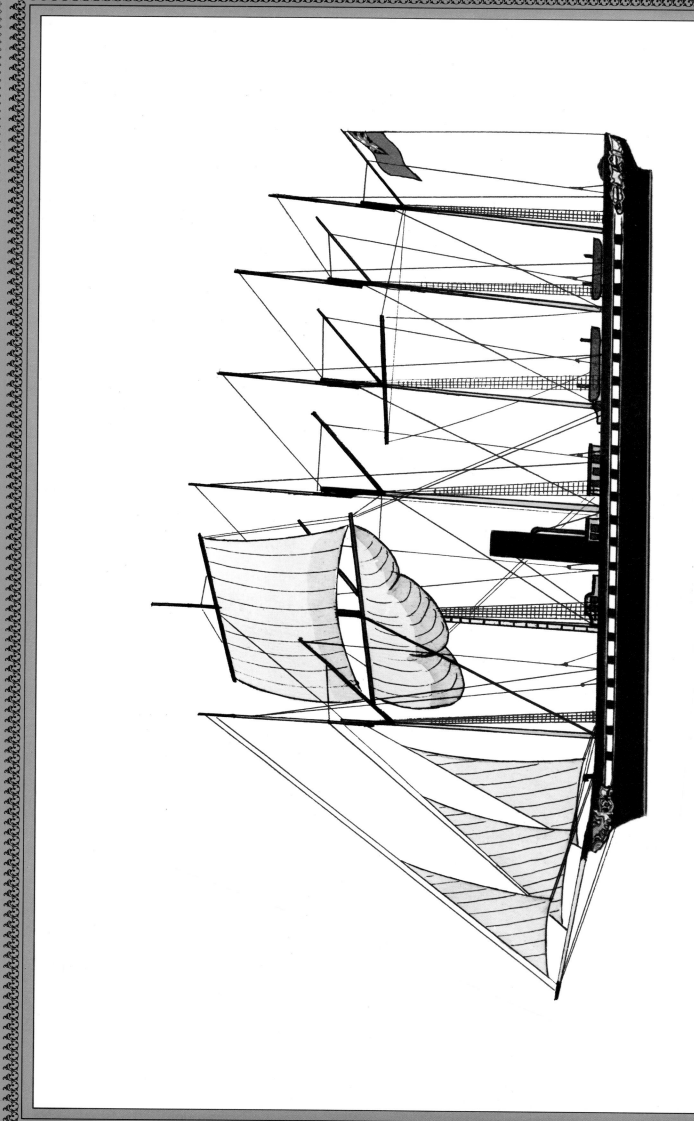

S.S. Great Britain

The Thermopylae

In the last years of the 1860s two composite clipper ships were launched which were to become famous.

The first of these, launched in 1868, was the *Thermopylae*, which was designed by Bernard Waymouth and built by Walter Hood of Aberdeen for the Aberdeen White Star Line. The ship was 212 feet long had a beam of 36 feet and a depth of just over 20 feet, with a raked stem and rounded forefoot. She had a deep false keel to give her more grip on the water. The sail plan was of particular interest as the main yard was 80 feet long.

The *Thermopylae* remained in the tea trade until 1881. After that she carried rice for a Canadian company and was then bought by the Portuguese government for use as a training ship. In her new role she was renamed the *Pedro Nunes*. Twelve years later, after a great career, she was sunk off the mouth of the Tagus River, with full naval honours.

PLATE XV

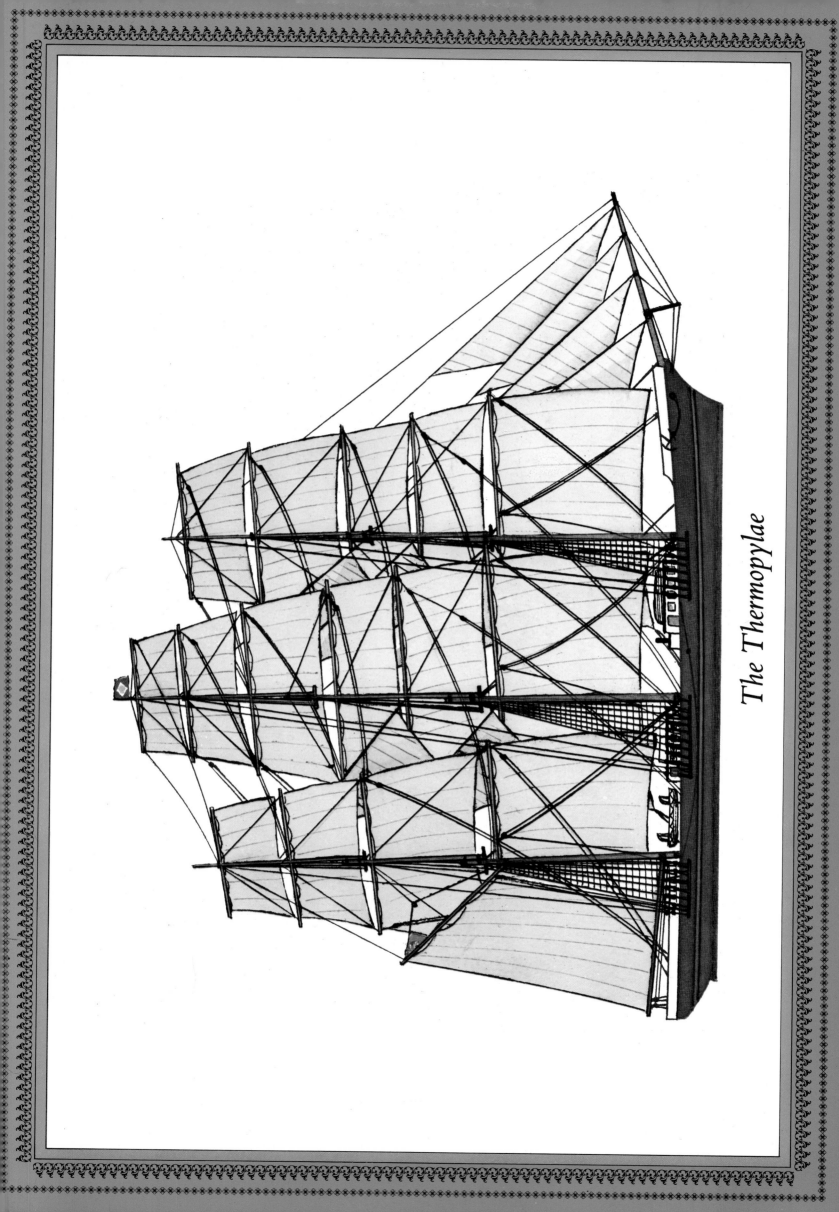

The Thermopylae

The Cutty Sark

The *Cutty Sark* was built as a rival to the *Thermopylae* and was designed by the naval architect Hercules Linton. She was built at the Dumbarton yard of Scott and Linton and was launched in November 1869.

Intended for the China tea trade, the ship had a length of 212 feet, a beam of 36 feet and a hold depth of 21 feet. She weighed 963 tons.

One of the most famous, if not *the* most famous clipper, *Cutty Sark* was used to carry wool when the tea trade collapsed, and it was during this period that she accomplished some of her fastest times. At one point she made a record journey from Sydney, Australia, to London in 71 days.

On one occasion the *Cutty Sark* was ahead of the *Thermopylae* in a race to transport cargo, when she lost her rudder in a heavy sea. The captain was not a man to give in easily to disaster, and a new rudder was made of spars and forged together on deck in raging seas, whereafter it was fitted to the ship in similarly bad weather. The *Cutty Sark* lost the race to the *Thermopylae* but at least got back to port unaided.

In 1953 the ship was taken over by the *Cutty Sark* Preservation Society, and today she is on show to the public in Greenwich dry-dock – the last British Clipper in history.

PLATE XVI

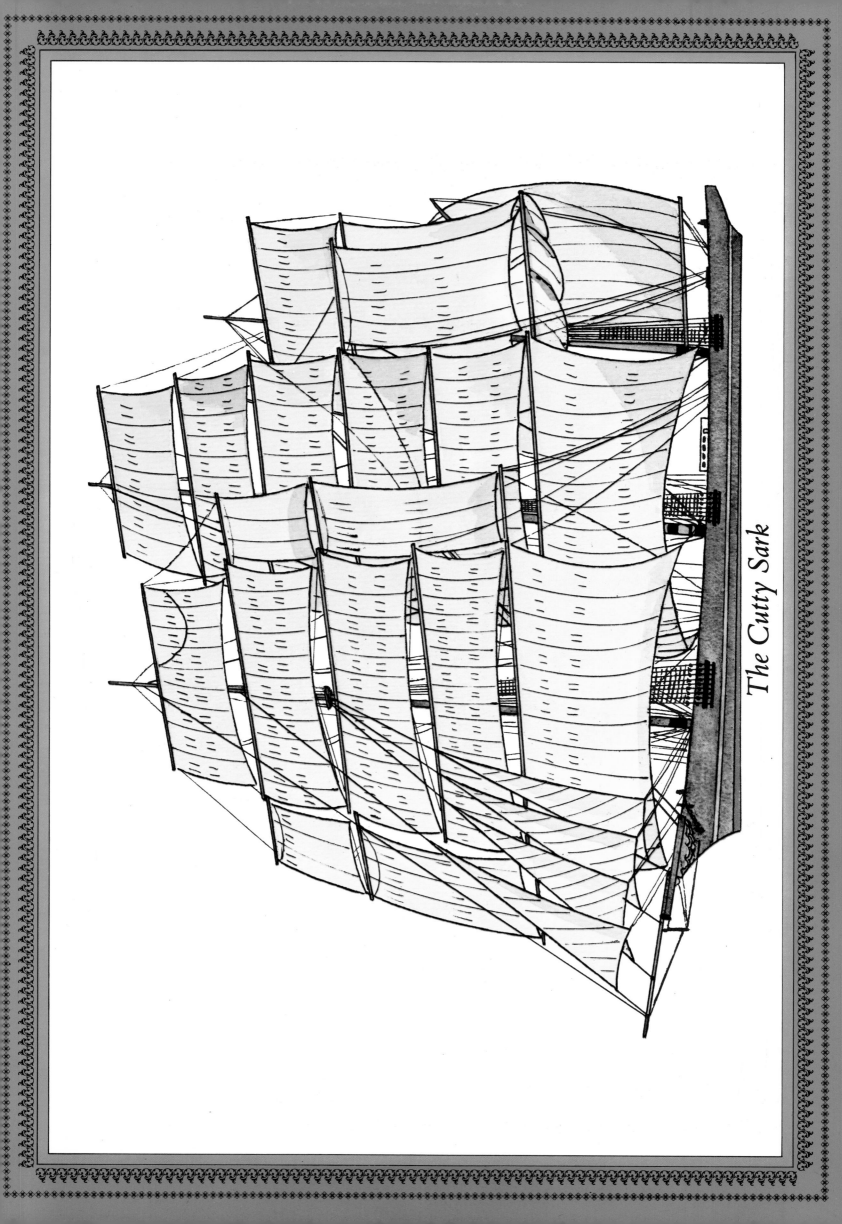

The Cutty Sark

The Port Jackson

The *Port Jackson* was another fine specimen of the type of ship referred to as 'Colonial clipper'. She spent most of her life sailing between London and Australia, taking emigrants on the outward passage and returning with cargoes of wool.

It can be seen how the hull of the clipper resembles closely that of present-day ships; it was designed with safety, speed, and efficiency foremost in mind.

Colonial clippers were sailed by men whose skills with rope and canvas were often pitted against the worst possible weather conditions.

PLATE XVII

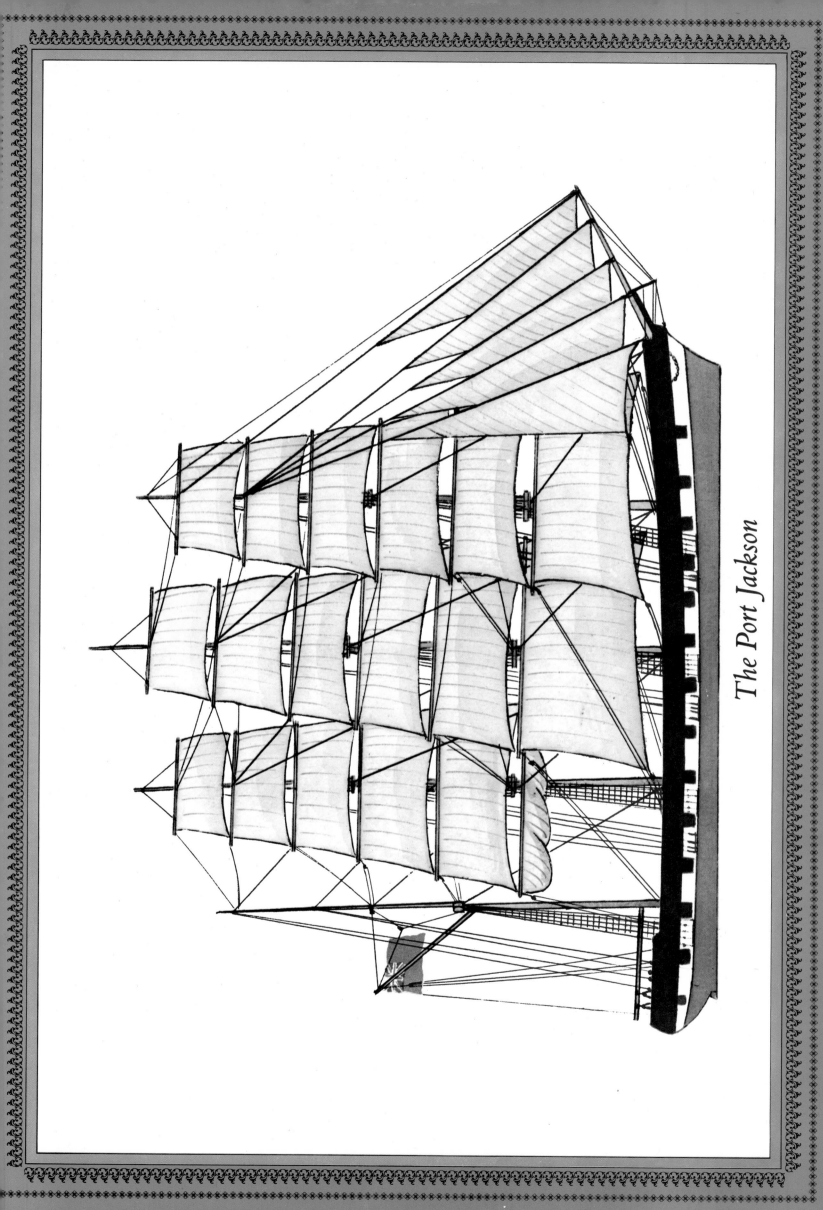

The Port Jackson

The Garthpool

The *Garthpool* was one of the very last British sailing ships. A four-masted barque, and commonly known as a 'windjammer', she ended England's world-wide trading where sailing ships were concerned. Of steel construction, and built in 1891 she had a net weight of 2,652 tons, a length of 310 feet, a beam of 45 feet and a depth of 25 feet.

Owned by the Marine Navigation Company of Canada, *Garthpool* sailed to almost every corner of the globe on the known trading routes and was the equivalent of our modern tramp steamer, sailing anywhere a cargo was available.

The final voyage for the *Garthpool* began from Hull in October 1929 when she was bound for Australia. From the commencement of this voyage bad weather, minor mishaps and damage delayed the ship's progress, until finally on the night of 11 November she ran aground on one of the Cape Verde Islands. The impact with the reef was so severe that the ship could not be backed off. The crew, under orders, abandoned the *Garthpool* which was rapidly breaking up; and after a hazardous journey the lifeboats made for Boarvista Island, where native craft rescued the shipwrecked men and took them ashore.

PLATE XVIII

The Garthpool

A Thames Barge

Developed during the middle of the nineteenth century as a specialized cargo carrier – and probably the most efficient and cheapest method of transport devised – Thames barges could be sailed by a crew of two men only and when fully laden had a draught of merely 6 feet. This shallow draught was due to the broad beam and flat bottom.

These barges were designed for work in the Thames Estuary, which has numerous shoals or sandbanks. Even if driven on to a sandbank, they remained perfectly stable.

PLATE XIX

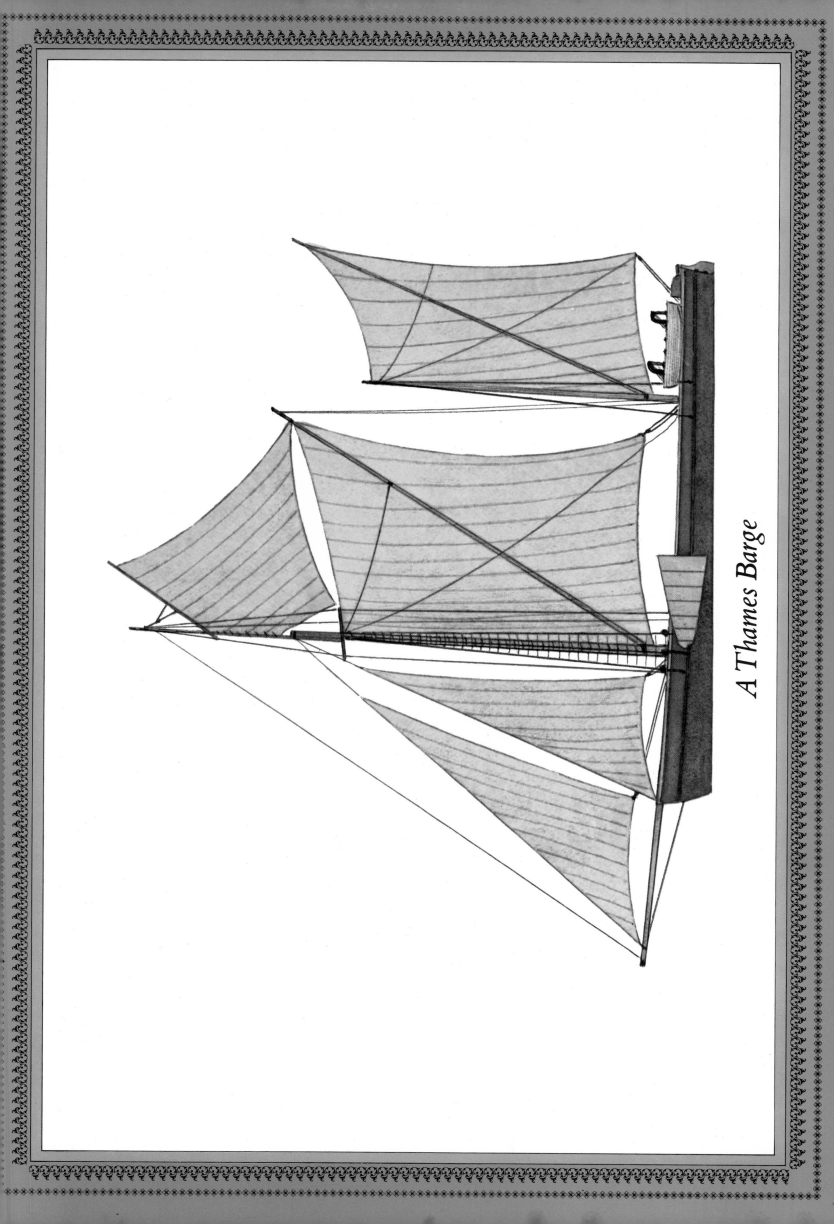

A Thames Barge

The Archibald Russell

Probably the best known of all British mercantile sailing ships, the four-masted steel barque *Archibald Russell* was built in 1905 by Scotts of Greenock. Weighing 2,385 tons, she was the last four-masted barque to be built for a British owner – J. Hardie & Company of Glasgow.

After a short life operating primarily as a grain ship, she was sold and joined in history other famous names such as the *Hezogin Cecilie*, *Moshula* and *Pamir*. Under her new owner and the Finnish flag she operated for some years again as a grain ship, then as a crew-training vessel.

PLATE XX

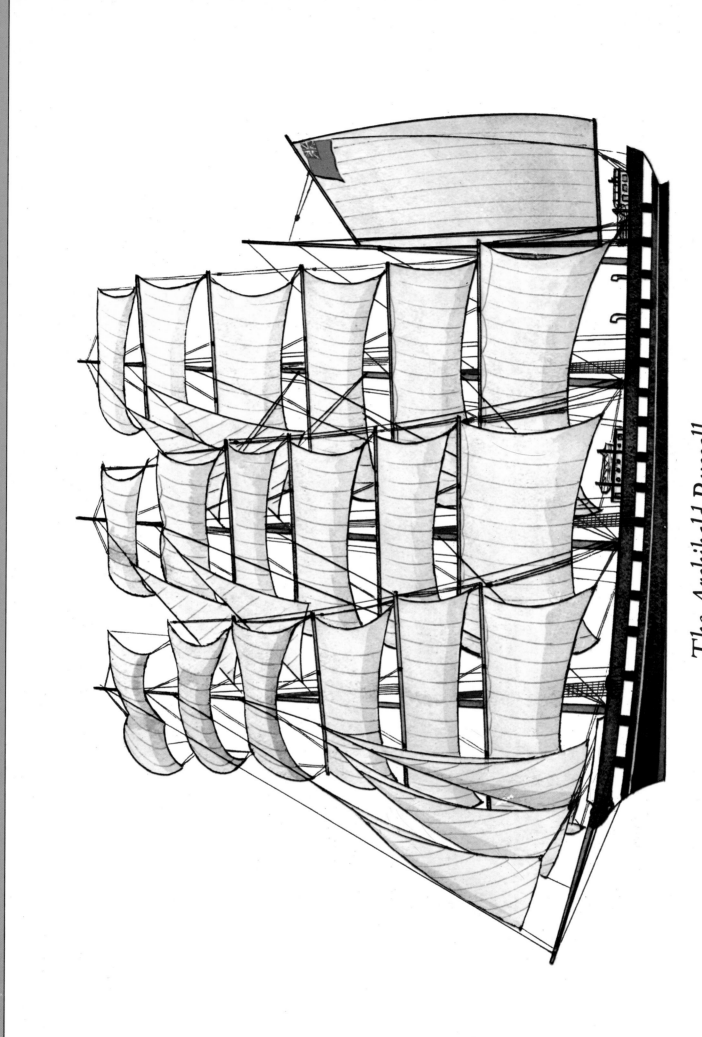

The Archibald Russell

The Discovery

The sixth exploration ship to be called the *Discovery* was built on the Tay at the end of the last century for Captain Scott's Antarctic expedition. The decision to perpetuate the name was decided at a meeting of the Royal Geographical Society in June 1900 and formally conferred by Lady Markham, when *Discovery* was launched on 21 March 1901 at Dundee.

The *Discovery* was purpose-built according to the design of W. E. Smith, one of the chief constructors at the Admiralty. Her frame was of solid English oak, 26 inches thick, and made to resist tremendous side stresses, while her bows were fortified to a degree beyond anything previously known in wooden-ship construction. Some of the bolts were 8 feet long, running entirely through wood.)

Discovery's stem was designed to crack a passage through pack ice: when she charged into the ice the fore part was lifted two or three feet until the ship's weight acted with a downward force that cracked the ice floe and made a passage for her to move through.

Captain Robert Falcon Scott left Cowes, Isle of Wight, in *Discovery* for his scientific expedition to the Antarctic and was the South Pole on 6 August 1901. His historic mission was concluded on 10 September 1904 when the ship sailed back to Southsea.

In 1906 *Discovery* was sold to the Hudson's Bay Company for £10,000, and was engaged in trading voyages until 1920.

In 1931 she was laid up in the East India Dock, London and remained there until 1937. She was then handed over to the Boy Scouts Association and towed to a mooring in the River Thames, where she remains to this day on exhibition to the public all year round.

PLATE XXI

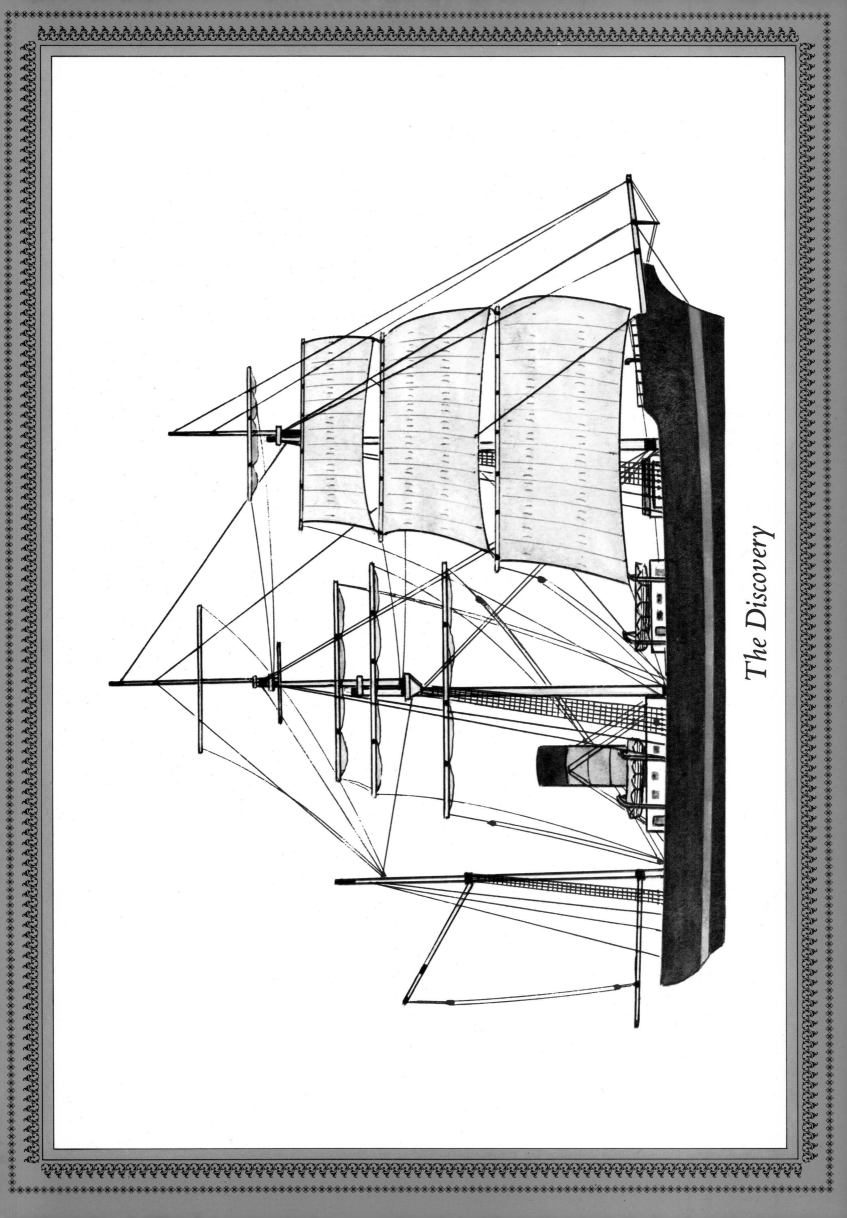

The Discovery

A Schooner

Now almost entirely disappeared from our coastal waters, the schooner was one of the most popular ships during the last hundred years. The illustration shows the Norman type of schooner used extensively up to the beginning of the First World War in 1914. The rig of the schooner varied considerably, and the ship depicted was classified as a topsail schooner, having two masts and square sails on the fore-topmast.

The topsail schooner was popular with the British maritime world for use round the coasts and trade with European ports – particularly in Britain's wine trade with Portugal.

As with all other sailing craft, the schooners had to give way to steam and motor ships. They could still be seen occasionally, however, right into the mid 1930s.

PLATE XXII

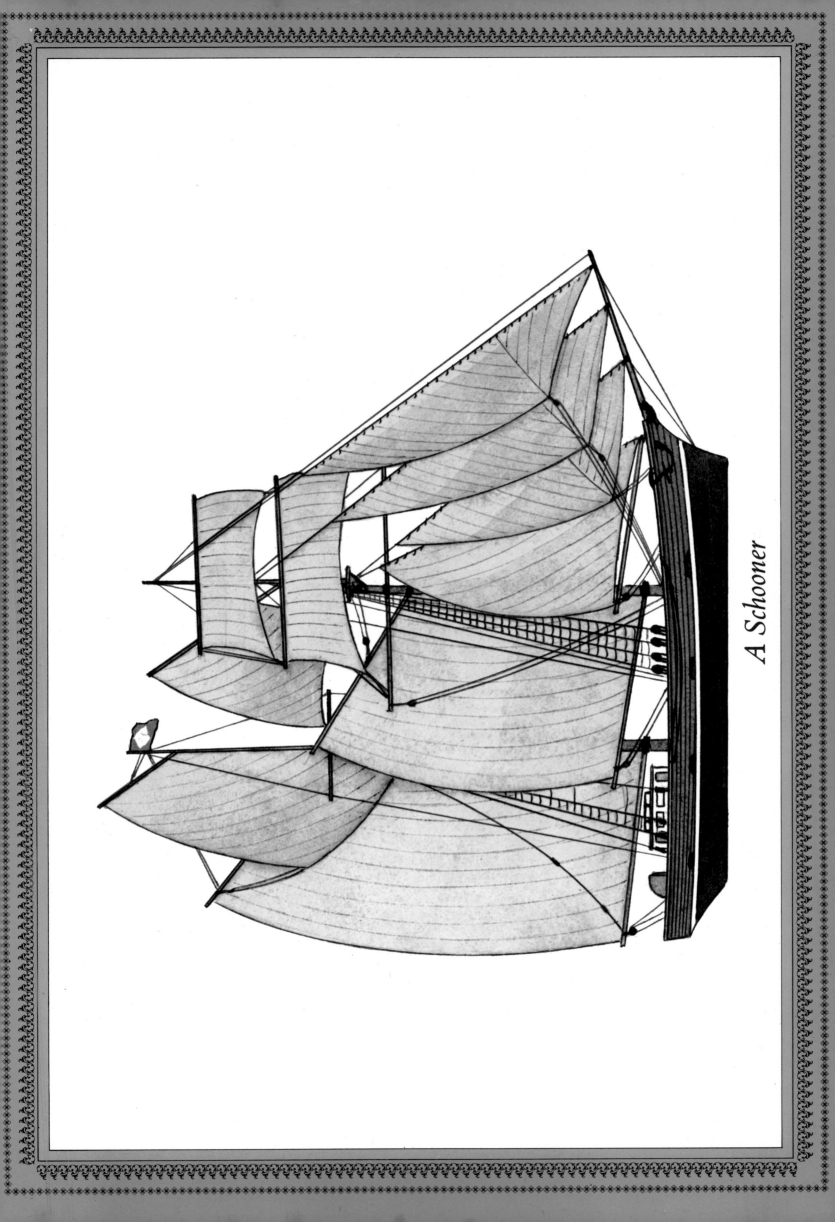

A Schooner

The Sir Winston Churchill

Owned by the Sail Training Association, the ship bearing this proud name was launched in 1966. The scheduled launch in the autumn of 1965 was delayed due to her being blown over on her side while still on the stocks.

The *Sir Winston Churchill* was acquired for the association as a means of enabling young people to gain experience in sail, live closely together, and create a sea fellowship. In all of these respects she has been successful. Her permanent crew consists of only six men, but on voyages this number is augmented by 40 young people.

Apart from sail, the ship is equipped with two 120-horsepower auxiliary engines, which give a speed of up to $9\frac{1}{2}$ knots; plus the most up-to-date navigational instruments and safety devices.

Built at the Hessle Yard in Yorkshire, the ship's leading dimensions are: displacement 281 tons, overall length 150 feet 5 inches, beam 26 feet 8 inches and draught 15 feet 9 inches.

Applications to sail on the ship have to be made by young people many months in advance of sailing dates – particularly when the vessel is a contestant in the Race for Tall Ships.

Her figurehead is a red lion, which is the symbol of the Sail Training Association, whose president is H.R.H. The Duke of Edinburgh.

PLATE XXIII

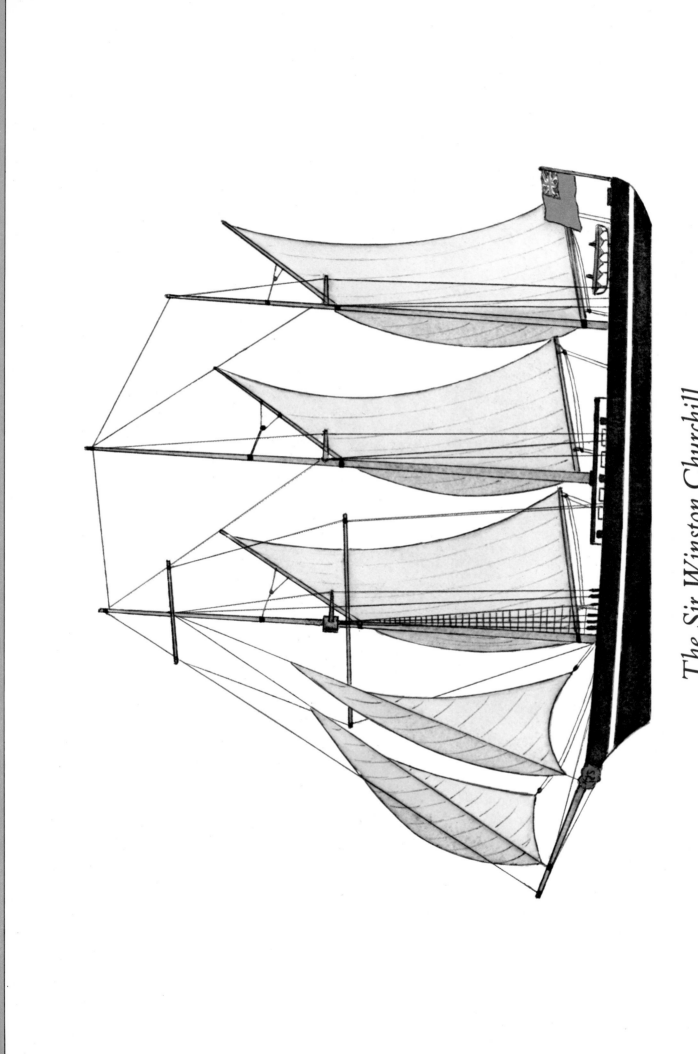

The Sir Winston Churchill

The British Steel

The British Steel Corporation sponsored the building of *British Steel* at the Phillips Yard, Dartmouth. She has an overall length of 59 feet, a beam width of 12 feet 10 inches, a draught of 8 feet and when fully laden a displacement of 17 tons.

Steel used in the construction was specially treated before and after building. Five tons of lead were incorporated in the keel to give stability and overcome out-of-balance forces created by 1,500 square feet of sail area.

British Steel became famous when Chay Blyth sailed her from Hamble, Hampshire, single-handed round the world in 292 days. The voyage was unique because Blyth sailed from east to west – the opposite direction to that in which the Trade Winds blow.

PLATE XXIV

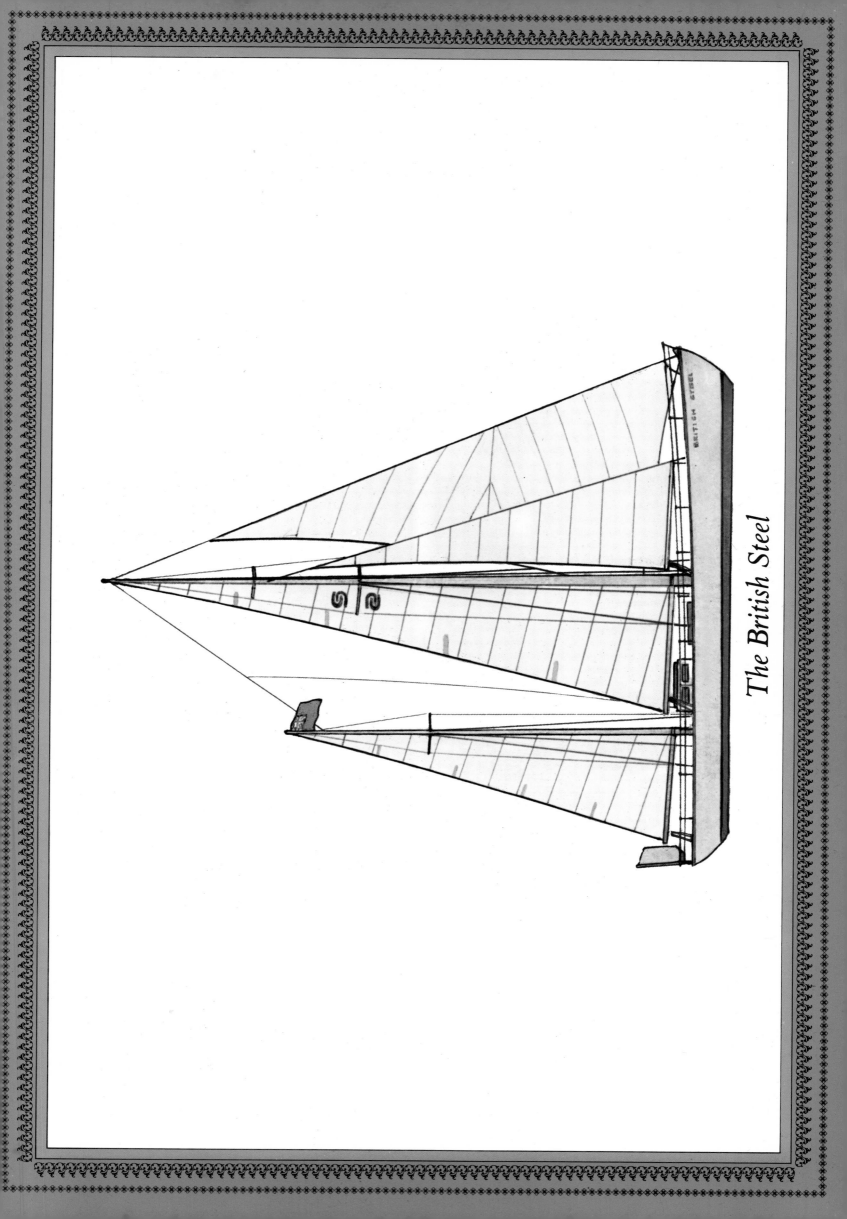

The British Steel